WORLD ENGLISH 3

THIRD EDITION

Real People · Real Places · Real Language

Christien Lee, Author

Kristin L. Johannsen and Rebecca Tarver Chase, Authors

NATIONAL GEOGRAPHIC
L E A R N I N G

Australia · Brazil · Mexico · Singapore · United Kingdom · United States

NATIONAL GEOGRAPHIC
L E A R N I N G

National Geographic Learning,
a Cengage Company

World English Level 3:
Real People, Real Places, Real Language
Christien Lee, Author
Kristin L. Johannsen and Rebecca Tarver Chase,
Authors

Publisher: Sherrise Roehr

Executive Editor: Sarah Kenney

Senior Development Editor: Margarita Matte

Media Researcher: Leila Hishmeh

Senior Technology Product Manager: Lauren Krolick

Director of Global Marketing: Ian Martin

Senior Product Marketing Manager:
  Caitlin Thomas

Heads of Regional Marketing:
  Charlotte Ellis (Europe, Middle East and Africa)
  Kiel Hamm (Asia)
  Irina Pereyra (Latin America)

Production Manager: Daisy Sosa

Senior Print Buyer: Mary Beth Hennebury

Art Director: Brenda Carmichael

Operations Support: Hayley Chwazik-Gee

Compositor: MPS Limited

For permission to use material from this text or product,
submit all requests online at **cengage.com/permissions**
Further permissions questions can be emailed to
permissionrequest@cengage.com

World English 3 ISBN: 978-0-357-11369-1
World English 3 + MyWorldEnglishOnline Workbook ISBN: 978-0-357-13026-1

National Geographic Learning
20 Channel Center Street
Boston, MA 02210
USA

Locate your local office at **international.cengage.com/region**

Visit our corporate website at **www.cengage.com**

Printed in China
Print Number: 05   Print Year: 2021

Thank you to the educators who provided invaluable feedback during the development of the third edition of the *World English* series:

AMERICAS

Brazil

Gabriely Billordo, Berlitz, Porto Alegre
Bruna Caltabiano, Caltabiano Idiomas, Sao Paulo
Sophia de Carvalho, Inglês Express, Belo Horizonte
Renata Coelho, 2b English for you, Florianopolis
Rebecca Ashley Hibas, Inglês Express, Belo Horizonte
Cristina Kobashi, Cultivar Escola de Idiomas, Guaratinguetá
Silvia Teles Barbosa, Colégio Cândido Portinari, Salvador

Chile

Jorge Cuevas, Universidad Santo Tomás, Los Angeles

Colombia

Ruben Cano, UPB University, Medellin
Javier Vega, Fundación Universitaria de Popayán, Popayán

Costa Rica

Jonathan Acuna, Centro Cultural Costarricense Americano, San José
Lilly Sevilla, Centro Cultural Costarricense Americano, San José

Mexico

Jose Aguirre, Instituto Tecnológico Superior de Irapuato, Salamanca
Alejandro Alvarado Cupil, Instituto Tecnológico de Minatitlán, Minatitlan
Jhosellin Angeles, ITSOEH, Mixquiahuala de Juárez, Hidalgo
René Bautista, BUAP, Puebla
Imelda Félix, Colegio Cervantes Costa Rica, Guadalajara
Isabel Fernández, Universidad Autónoma de Aguascalientes, Aguascalientes
Andres Garcia, FES Aragon (UNAM), Mexico City
Jessica Garcia, Colegio Cultural, Puebla
Lazaro Garcia, Tecnológico de Toluca, Metepec
Fernando Gómez, Universidad Tecnológica Jalisco,Guadalajara
Alma Gopar, FES Zaragoza (UNAM), Mexico City
Inés Gutierrez, University of Colima, Colima
Jesus Chavez Hernandez, Universidad Aeronáutica en Querétaro, Colón
Cristina Mendez, Instituto Tecnológico Superior de Irapuato, Irapuato
Elena Mioto, UNIVA, Guadalajara
Rubén Mauricio Muñoz Morales, Universidad Santo Tomás, Villavicencio
Maria Rodríguez, Universidad Aeronáutica en Querétaro, Colón
Ana Lilia Terrazas, ICO, Puebla

United States

Amy Fouts, Face to Face Learning Center, Doral, FL
Virginia Jorge, UCEDA International, New Brunswick, NJ
Richard McDorman, Language On, Miami, FL
Sarah Mikulski, Harper College, Palatine, IL
Rachel Scheiner, Seattle Central College, Seattle, WA
Pamela Smart-Smith, Virginia Tech Language and Culture Institute, Blacksburg, VA
Marcie Stone, American English College, Rowland Heights, CA
Colin Ward, Lone Star College-North Harris, Houston, TX
Marla Yoshida, University of California, Irvine, CA

ASIA

Nazarul Azali, UiTM Cawangan Melaka, Alor Gajah
Steven Bretherick, Tohoku Fukushi University, Sendai
Sam Bruce, Soka University, Hachioji
Karen Cline-Katayama, Hokusei Gakuen University and Tokai University, Sapporo
Tom David, Japan College of Foreign Languages, Tokyo
Johnny Eckstein, Soka University, Hachioji
Meg Ellis, Kyoto Tachibana University, Kyoto
Thomas Goetz, Hokusei Gakuen University, Sapporo
Katsuko Hirai, Matsuyama University, Matsuyama
Paul Horness, Soka University, Hachioji
David Kluge, Nanzan University, Nagoya
Stephen Lambacher, Aoyama Gakuin University, Tokyo
Yi-An Lin, National Taipei University of Business, Taipei
Kerry McCatty, Soka University, Hachioji
Gregg McNabb, Shizuoka Institute of Technology, Shizuoka
Collin Mehmet, Matsumoto University, Matsumoto City
Sean Mehmet, Shinshu University, Matsumoto
Lin Mingying, Soka University, Hachioji
Erika Nakatsuka, Soka University, Hachioji
Seiko Oguri, Chubu University, Nagoya
Thomas Nishikawa, Ritsumeikan University, Kyoto
Sean Otani, Tottori University, Tottori
Daniel Paller, Kinjo Gakuin University, Nagoya
Tomomi Sasaki, Ibaraki University, Mito
Mark Shrosbree, Tokai University, Hiratsuka
Brent Simmons, Aichi Gakuin University, Nagoya
Mikiko Sudo, Soka University, Hachioji
Monika Szirmai, Hiroshima International University, Hiroshima
Matthew Taylor, Kinjo Gakuin University, Nagoya
James Thomas, Kokusai Junior College, Tokyo
Asca Tsushima, Soka University, Hachioji
Hui Chun Yu, Macau University of Science and Technology, Macau

Listening	Speaking and Pronunciation	Reading	Writing	Video Journal
Focused Listening A Discussion: Migration Factors	Discussing Reasons for Staying or Moving Describing an Ideal Place to Live Contractions with Auxiliary Verbs	Quality of Life	Writing a Paragraph Describing a City	**The World's Biggest Melting Pot** In this National Geographic video, we learn about the benefits of living in a multicultural city.
Listening for General Understanding and Specific Information An Interview: Cognitive Biases	Discussing Mental Influences Describing Emotions *Th* Sounds	How Memories are Made	Writing about an Emotional Experience	**Can You Really Tell If a Kid Is Lying?** In this TED Talk, Kang Lee explains the effect of telling lies in children.
General and Focused Listening An Interview: Extreme Weather Events	Discussing Cause and Effect Talking about Slogans Linking Words Together	Is Coffee in Danger?	Writing a Summary of Your Ideas	**Tales of Ice-bound Wonderlands** In this TED Talk, Paul Nicklen explains how a changing ecosystem can hurt the animals that live there.
General and Focused Listening A Conversation: Life-Changing Moments	Discussing Important People or Events Expressing Agreement and Disagreement Saying *To*	Want a Better Job? Work for a Better Company	Writing an Opinion Paragraph	**A Life Lesson from a Volunteer Firefighter** In this TED Talk, Mark Bezos describes how every act of generosity matters.
General and Focused Listening A Talk: Types of Fossils	Talking about the Survival of Species Giving Advice about Difficult Situations Emphasis to Express Meaning	A Birthday to Remember	Writing a Paragraph Giving Advice	**Three Things I Learned While My Plane Crashed** In this TED Talk, Ric Elias explains how your life can be changed by an event.
Listening for General Understanding A Radio Call-in Show: Public Art	Discussing Opinions about Art Talking about Profiles of Artists Thought Groups	The Art Bubble	Writing a Biographical Profile	**Antarctica: While You Were Sleeping** In this National Geographic Short Film Showcase video, Joseph Michael describes how art can raise awareness of issues related to Antarctica.

Listening	Speaking and Pronunciation	Reading	Writing	Video Journal
Focused Listening An Interview: Self-Driving Vehicles	Talking about Transportation Discussing Reviews Reduced Auxiliaries *Are* and *Have*	The Future of "Travel"?	Writing a Review	**SpaceX's Plan to Fly You across the Globe in 60 Minutes** In this TED Talk, Gwynne Shotwell explains why space travel, as a way to travel around the world, is possible.
Listening for General Understanding and Specific Information A Radio Interview: Running a Marathon	Discussing Competition Comparing and Contrasting Two Topics Intonation and Emphasis to Express Attitude	When Losing Means Winning	Writing a Compare and Contrast Text	**What I Learned When I Conquered the World's Toughest Triathlon** In this TED Talk, Minda Dentler describes the personal challenges of a triathlon competition.
Focused and General Listening A Radio Interview: The Job of a Stunt Person	Talking about Dangerous Jobs Giving Clear Instructions Consonant Clusters	Is Too Much Safety a Risk?	Writing Clear Instructions	**An Everyday Danger** In this National Geographic video, we learn about the difficulties of living with allergies.
Listening for General Understanding A Conversation: Discussing Historical Figures	Talking about Studying the Past Describing Mysterious Objects Intonation for Lists	Back to the Moon?	Writing a Description	**From Ancient to Modern** In this National Geographic video, we learn how ancient cultures have influenced our contemporary culture.
Listening for General Understanding A Talk: Research into the Experience of Learning	Talking about Learning Describing Problems and Solutions Enunciation	Games: More Than Just Fun	Writing an Email Giving Suggestions	**Sola Power** In this National Geographic video, Shabana Basij-Rasikh explains the importance of education for girls.
General and Focused Listening A Podcast: Competition and Innovation	Talking about Positive Outcomes Discussing Purposes and Results Stress in Compound Nouns	Daily Habits of Successful Innovators	Writing about Purpose and Results	**Why You Should Make Useless Things** In this TED Talk, Simone Giertz describes how playing and asking questions can lead to innovation.

Where We Live

Houses covered in
snow in Freudenberg,
Germany

UNIT 1 GOALS

A. Talk about How Long or How Often

B. Discuss Why People Move

C. Give Reasons and Explain Results

D. Discuss Improving Communities

E. Describe Places to Live

GOAL Talk about How Long or How Often

Vocabulary

A Read the messages.

Performers doing a lion dance share Chinese culture in the Chinatown neighborhood of Boston, MA, US

Hi Emily,

How are you? I hope you and your family are well. My wife and I have been talking about moving to your city. There are several factors, but the main reason is that we want a better quality of life. You've lived there for many years. Do you think it's a good place to live?

Pablo

Hi Pablo,

Lovely to hear from you, Pablo. I'm excited that you've been thinking of moving here. Like many residents, I think there are many great communities in the city. About half of the population comes from different cultures from around the world, so it's an exciting, multicultural place. It's not perfect, though. Most neighborhoods are nice, but some are dirty with a lot of trash on the streets. And these days, people are less friendly and don't try to help each other. I guess society has changed a lot since we were kids! Anyway, before you make a decision, read books on migration problems. I've read several, and they have some good advice.

Emily

B Complete each sentence with the singular form of a blue word or phrase from the messages.

1. A _____community_____ is a group of people who live in one part of a city or a country.

2. _____ is when many people move from one place to another.

3. _____ means all of the people who live in one area, city, or country.

4. _____ means how good or bad life is in one place or for one person.

5. _____ is what people throw away.

6. _____ is a general way to refer to people in a country or in the world.

7. A _____ is a group of people who think and act in similar ways.

8. A _____ is a reason for something or a cause of something.

9. A _____ is one area within a city.

10. A _____ is somebody who lives in a place, such as a city or country.

C In his message, Pablo says he might move to find a better quality of life. In small groups, discuss what things can lead to a good quality of life.

Grammar

Present Perfect and Present Perfect Continuous

The present perfect (*has / have* + past participle) and the present perfect continuous (*has / have* + *been* + present participle) both refer to past situations connected to the present.	I **have lived** here for a long time. I**'ve been living** here for a long time.
In most cases, use the present perfect rather than the present perfect continuous: **1.** to emphasize that an event is finished. **2.** to describe things that happened at an unspecified time in the past	**1.** He **has told** us already. **2.** She**'s** just **started** a new job.
In most cases, use the present perfect continuous rather than the present perfect: **1.** to emphasize how long something continued. **2.** to describe past actions that are still continuing.	**1.** They**'ve been waiting** for hours. **2.** It **has been raining** since yesterday.
Some time expressions are common with both forms: **1.** Use *for* to say how long something has continued. **2.** Use *since* to indicate when something started.	**1.** We**'ve worked** together *for* years. **2.** We**'ve been working** together *since* 2015.

D Underline examples of the present perfect and present perfect continuous in the emails in **A**.

E Complete these sentences with the correct form (present perfect, present perfect continuous, or both) of the verb in parentheses.

1. Emily _____ (live) in the same city since 2015.

2. Mark _____ (finish) reading the book already.

3. Thiago _____ (stop) using social media so much.

4. It _____ (snow) nonstop for the last seven hours.

5. Jin-hwa and Hye-rim _____ (be) friends for years.

F In pairs, compare your answers in **E**. Then take turns saying the sentences.

 GOAL CHECK Talk About How Long or How Often

In small groups, take turns asking and answering these questions. Then vote on the most interesting answer to each question and share them with the class.

1. What is one thing you've been doing for many years but dislike? Why do you keep doing it?

2. What is one thing you've already done several times today? Why have you done it so often?

3. What is one thing you've recently finished? How long did it take you? How do you feel now?

4. Who is one person you've known for less than a year? How often have you seen this person?

B GOAL Discuss Why People Move

Listening

A You are going to hear an academic discussion about migration *push* and *pull* factors. Before you listen, complete these definitions in pairs.

Migration push factors are negative things that _____.
In contrast, pull factors are positive things that _____.

B 🎧 2 Listen to the first part of the discussion and check your definitions.

C 🎧 3 Listen to the whole discussion and take notes. Then write *cultural*, *economic*, *environmental*, or *personal*.

1. Put the factors in the order the professor mentions them.

1: _____ factors
2: _____ factors
3: _____ factors
4: _____ factors

2. Write the correct factor for each example that the speakers mention.

- bad family relationship: _____ factor

- excellent quality of life: _____ factor

- good or bad weather: _____ factor

- high house prices: _____ factor

D In groups, decide if the examples below are *cultural, economic, environmental,* or *personal* and whether each would be a *push* or *pull* factor. Then think of an opposite example.

- a natural disaster that affects a country
- poor schools and colleges in an area
- high average salaries in one large city
- having many friends who live nearby

E **MY WORLD** Think of a place you know well. Then in groups, talk about its biggest *push* and *pull* factors.

PRONUNCIATION: Contractions with Auxiliary Verbs

In speech and informal writing, it is common to use the contracted form of auxiliaries like *be, have, would,* and *will*.

Auxiliary	Contraction(s)	Example
am / is / are	'm / 's / 're	She**'s** moving overseas next month.
has / have / had	's / 've / 'd	I**'ve** been looking for a new job.
would	'd	They**'d** like to emigrate to Canada.
will	'll	He**'ll** call us tomorrow.

F 🎧 4　Write the contractions. Then listen and check (✓) the ones you hear.

1. … we have discussed … _____ ☐
2. … I am going to … _____ ☐
3. … they are different … _____ ☐
4. … I would like … _____ ☐
5. … he has finished … _____ ☐
6. … I will leave … _____ ☐
7. … my sister is kind of … _____ ☐
8. … we had moved … _____ ☐

G In pairs, take turns saying the contractions in **F** aloud. Then take turns making new sentences using the contractions.

Communication

H Read the information in the box. Then, in small groups, complete the tasks.

> Some factors do not push people away from a place or pull people to a place. Instead, they make people want to stay in the place where they already live.

1. Come up with a good name for these factors.
2. Make a list of some examples of these factors.
3. Share your ideas with the class. Vote on the best name.

✓ **GOAL CHECK** Discuss why people move

Think about the last time you moved somewhere (either on your own or with your family). Then, in pairs, take turns saying where you moved from and to. What push and pull factors were reasons for the move? How long you have lived in the new place? What factors make you want to stay in the new place?

People explore Bolívar Square in Bogotá, Colombia. Good weather makes Colombia an attractive place to live in or visit.

C GOAL Give Reasons and Explain Results

Language Expansion: Where You're From

A Complete the information with the phrases in the box. Use one phrase twice.

country name

nationality adjective

To talk about your background, you can say *I'm …* plus a
(1) _____. For example, *I'm Brazilian.* Alternatively,
you can say *I'm from … / I was born in … / I come from …* plus a
(2) _____. For example, *I'm from Brazil.* If your
parents or grandparents come from more than one country, you can
describe your background using words like *half* or *quarter* and a
(3) _____. For example, *I'm half Brazilian and half Japanese.*

B 🎧 5 Listen to the conversation.

Tom: I'm doing some research about family histories. Could you tell me about your background?

Julia: Sure! I have a diverse background. I was born here, but my mom comes from Mexico, and my dad's from Brazil, but his parents were born in Japan. So I guess I'm half Mexican, one-quarter Brazilian, and one-quarter Japanese.

Tom: Wow! Your family's really multicultural. Why did your parents choose to come here?

Julia: They thought that the quality of life here was so high that they should immigrate.

Tom: This city *does* have a good quality of life, but it's really expensive. I get so little money from my job that it's hard to live here.

Julia: You're right. House prices are rising so quickly that I've been thinking about moving somewhere cheaper.

Liberdade in São Paulo, Brazil is home to the largest Japanese community outside of Japan.

C In small groups, spend three minutes writing a list of as many country names and their nationality adjectives as you can. Share your list with another group. Whose list is longest?

D **MY WORLD** In different groups, take turns talking about where you are from. Who has the most diverse background?

Grammar

So … that
One way to give reasons and explain the result of something is to use *so… (that)* + a clause. The word(s) after *so* give the reason, and the clause after *that* explains the result. (Note: *that* is optional.)

Several *so … that* patterns are possible:	
1. *so* + adjective phrase (+ *that*) + clause	1. The movie is **so good that** I've seen it three times.
2. *so* + adverb phrase (+ *that*) + clause	2. She left **so quickly that** we couldn't say goodbye.
3. *so* + *many / few* + countable noun phrase (+ *that*) + clause	3. There are **so many good jobs in this city that** thousands of people have moved here.
4. *so* + *much / little* + uncountable noun phrase (+ *that*) + clause	4. I have **so little money this month that** I cannot even take the bus to work.

E In pairs, find the examples of *so … that* in the conversation. Match each example to one of the patterns in the grammar chart.

F Interview your classmates to complete these sentences. Then share your sentences with the class.

Example: _____*Claudia*_____ is so good at _____*science*_____ that _____*she won a competition*_____.

1. _____ is so busy these days that _____ _____.

2. _____ can _____ so well that _____.

3. _____ has so few _____ that _____.

4. _____ has so much _____ that _____.

 GOAL CHECK Give Reasons and Explain Results

Cut a piece of paper into ten equal pieces. On five of the pieces, write the *so* part of a *so … that* sentence; on the other five pieces, write the *that* part of the sentence. Then work in small groups. Can your partners correctly match your *so* phrases (reasons) and *that* phrases (results)?

GOAL Discuss Improving Communities

Reading

A Discuss the questions in small groups.

1. What is the man in the photo doing and how does it improve his community?

2. What other things can people do to improve their community?

B Scan the text. In which paragraph(s) do you find the following information?

1. The names of more than one company

2. The names of towns and cities

3. The names of people who started a trend

4. A description of a new kind of exercise

5. Ways to measure a city's quality of life

6. Some types of food that people are growing

7. The number of groups doing something

C Read the text. Circle uses of the present perfect. Then <u>underline</u> uses of *so ... that* in the text.

D In small groups, discuss where each benefit fits best in the diagram and why.

a. Lets local people spend time outdoors

b. Might help local residents save money

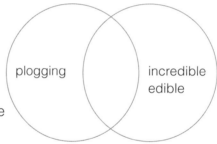

c. Makes communities more attractive

d. Could help local people become healthier

e. Has become popular all over the world

Plogging is a Scandinavian lifestyle trend where joggers pick up garbage as they run.

 GOAL CHECK

Think of a community that you know well. Then complete the steps.

1. List the community's push and pull factors.

2. How can you strengthen one pull factor or weaken one push factor to improve the community?

3. Share your ideas in small groups.

4. Whose idea was the best? Share your choice with the class.

Quality of Life

1   Each year, several organizations publish a list of world cities with the best quality of life. These organizations include the Economist Group and the magazine *Monocle*. Recently, cities like Melbourne in Australia, Vienna in Austria, Tokyo in Japan, and Vancouver in Canada have been on these lists. The organizations look at various factors to make their lists. For example, cities with a good quality of life usually have a stable government, little crime, and good public transportation and hospitals. They are also usually close to nature, have attractive buildings, access to museums, nice weather, and a clean environment.

2   For residents of these cities, life is generally great. However, even the best cities have some issues. In addition, approximately half of the world's population lives in cities with a lower quality of life. These people may dream of migrating somewhere better, but this may not be possible. A more practical alternative is for these people to find a way to improve the quality of life in their own communities.

3   Erik Ahlström provides a good example of this kind of personal action. Several years ago, he moved to Stockholm, the capital of Sweden. In general, Stockholm has an excellent quality of life. However, Ahlström felt that there was too much trash on the city streets. He decided to combine picking up the trash with jogging. He called this new activity *plogging*, and soon other people were helping him. Ahlström's idea for cleaning up the streets and parks of his community is simple. However, it has become so popular that people now go plogging in communities all over the world.

4   Mary Clear and Pam Warhurst are also good examples. They live in Todmorden, a small town in northern England. It's a nice place to live, but the two women wanted it to be even nicer. They found some areas of land nobody was using and began growing vegetables, fruit, and herbs. Their idea was that local residents could pick and eat them. People from other places soon heard about this "incredible **edible**" idea and wanted to know more. Todmorden now has so many visitors that residents there joke that they have invented a new form of tourism called *vegetable tourism*. Nowadays, at least 500 groups in places all over the world have started doing the same thing to improve their communities.

edible something you can eat

Communication

A Think about a place you would really like to live, such as a peaceful village in the countryside or an exciting, modern city like Bogotá. Make a list of the top five things you would want that place to have.

B Interview your classmates. Find someone whose list includes at least three things that are also on your list. Discuss why these things are important to you both.

C Interview your classmates again. Find someone whose list includes at least three things that are *not* on your list. Ask questions to find out why these things are important to him or her.

Writing

WRITING SKILL: Describing Something

One common goal for writing or speaking is to describe something to other people. A good description will help readers or listeners get a clear picture of something in their minds. There are several good ways to include descriptive language:

• use adjectives to describe nouns (e.g., a **large**, **exciting**, **modern** city)

• use adverbs to describe verbs or adjectives (e.g., the house is **beautifully** designed)

• use prepositional phrases to add details (e.g., a beautiful view **of the river**)

• make comparisons with other things (e.g., it's **larger than** a soccer field)

In pairs, match the underlined examples in the text about Bogotá to the different ways to include descriptive language mentioned in the Writing Skill box. Then find and underline more examples of descriptive language.

Bogotá is the <u>largest city</u> in Colombia and the capital <u>of that country</u>. It is a city with a long history. People <u>first started</u> living there in 1538. These days, it is a <u>multicultural city</u> with a population of around eight million people. Bogotá is more popular with tourists than other cities in Colombia. Tourists can easily travel around the city using the effective bus system. They can enjoy eating delicious food, visiting interesting museums, and spending time in Bogotá's many cool neighborhoods, such as La Candelaria or Zona Rosa.

✓ GOAL CHECK Describe Places to Live

Write a one-paragraph description of a place to live. Complete these steps in order.

Step 1: Choose the place you live now, a place you have lived before, or a place you would like to live in the future.

Step 2: Prepare to write the description. Use the checklist.

☐ Make notes about some ideas to include

☐ Decide what information from your notes to include

☐ Decide the best order in which to include this information

☐ Review the guide to writing descriptive language

Step 3: Write a first draft of your description.

Step 4: In pairs, read each other's first draft and give feedback to improve your partner's description.

Step 5: Write a final draft and submit your description.

Street performers getting ready to perform in Bogotá, Colombia

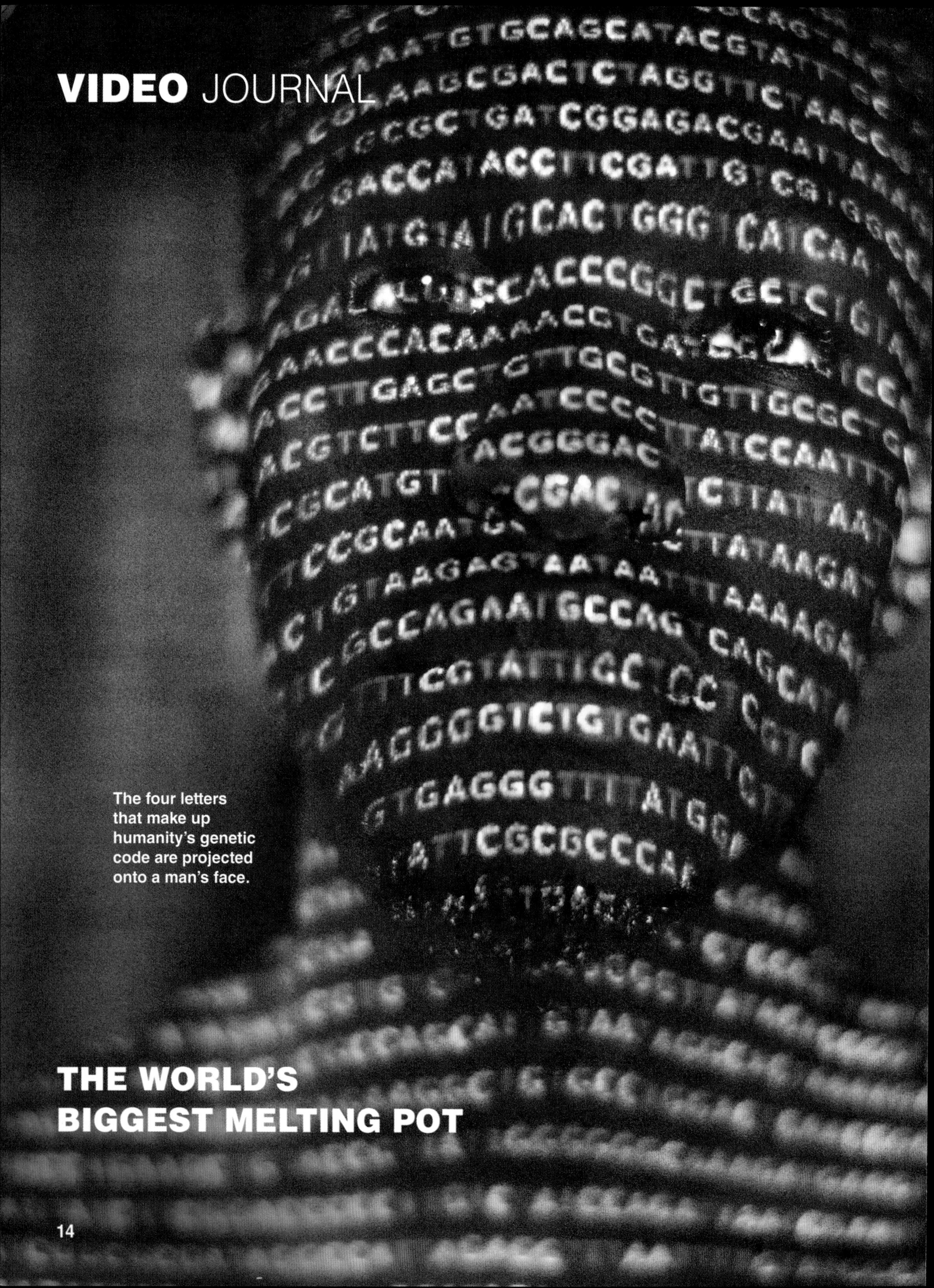

The four letters
that make up
humanity's genetic
code are projected
onto a man's face.

THE WORLD'S
BIGGEST MELTING POT

A Complete the survey of multicultural places by checking (✓) the boxes. Then, in pairs, compare answers and give reasons for your opinions.

	I've already visited	I'd like to visit	I don't want to visit
Amsterdam	☐	☐	☐
Dubai	☐	☐	☐
London	☐	☐	☐
New York City	☐	☐	☐
São Paulo	☐	☐	☐
Singapore	☐	☐	☐
Sydney	☐	☐	☐
Toronto	☐	☐	☐

B In small groups, discuss why people from many cultures move to multicultural places like the ones in **A**. What are some benefits of living in a multicultural place?

C Watch the video. Complete each statement with one word or number that you hear. Then watch again to confirm your answers.

1. According to a _____ of world records, Queens is the most multicultural place in the world.

2. Residents of Queens speak many languages and come from about _____ different countries.

3. Queens is an unusual multicultural place because no _____ or nationality is a majority.

4. A study from the year _____ showed that Queens is the most diverse place in the US.

5. Because it is so diverse, Queens is a good example of a melting _____.

D Match these metaphors for describing immigration to the correct definition.

a. _____ Melting pot

b. _____ Salad bowl

1. Immigrants combine well with the main culture of their new home, but also keep many parts of their original culture.

2. Immigrants become part of and add to the main culture of their new home, but lose most of their original culture.

E Discuss these questions in pairs.

1. In the video, Queens is described as a melting pot. Do you think a salad bowl is a better metaphor? Why?

2. Does either metaphor—a melting pot or a salad bowl—describe your country? Why?

F In new pairs, discuss and check (✓) which statements the residents of Queens from the video would probably agree with.

1. ☐ It is good to live in a multicultural neighborhood such as Queens.

2. ☐ It is good for a majority of people in a city to come from one culture.

3. ☐ It is good for everyone in a community to speak the same language.

4. ☐ It is good to learn about and be proud of one's family background.

G In small groups, discuss which statements in **F** you agree with most strongly.

15

UNIT

2

The Mind's Eye

An eastern screech
owl in its nest

Look at the photo and answer the questions.

1 What can you see in the photo?

2 Is it easy to understand the image, or did it take you a moment?

UNIT 2 GOALS

A. Express Degrees of Liking

B. Discuss Mental Influences

C. Talk about Personal Characteristics

D. Discuss Improving Your Memory

E. Describe an Emotional Experience

17

GOAL Express Degrees of Liking

Vocabulary

A Read the text. Then, in small groups, discuss which stage of life is most interesting for a child, and why.

Teenagers (ages 13–19) tend to take more risks than people of other ages.

Humans go through many physical changes from childhood to adulthood. For example, a baby boy might weigh 6 lb. and be less than 20 in. at birth, but might grow to 265 lb. and 6.5 ft. tall by the age of 20. In addition, people go through many mental changes. In fact, in some ways, the development of our minds is greater and more important than the growth of our bodies.

Here are some important cognitive milestones that all children go through:

0 to 11 months	• Can recognize the faces of family members • Can respond to facial expressions like smiles • Begin to connect words to objects or pictures
1 to 3 years	• Can follow instructions from adults or caregivers • Can imagine and make up stories or play imaginary games • May begin to tell lies about things they did or did not do
4 to 8 years	• Can recognize basic emotions like happiness in other people • May find that the actions of their friends can affect them • Can use more than one method to solve problems or puzzles
9 to 12 years	• May like to set a physical or mental challenge for themselves • Can understand that their actions may have long-term effects
13 to 17 years	• Can detect most emotions, such as disgust or shock, in others • Can understand and influence the beliefs of other people

WORD FOCUS

Cognitive milestones are important steps in a child's mental development.

B Complete these definitions with a blue word from the text.

1. _____ are opinions that people hold strongly.

2. _____ is the process of growing and changing.

3. _____ means related to the body, not the mind.

4. _____ means related to the mind, not the body.

5. A _____ is a hard task that requires a lot of work.

6. A _____ is a special way of doing something.

7. To _____ something means to change or influence it.

8. To _____ something means to create a picture of it in your mind.

9. To _____ something means to notice it or discover it.

10. To _____ two things means to join them or see how they are linked.

C In pairs, expand your vocabulary by writing the noun forms of *connect*, *detect*, and *imagine*; the verb forms of *challenge*, *development*, and *belief*; and the adverb forms of *mental* and *physical*. Use a dictionary if necessary.

Grammar

Infinitives and *-ing* Forms 1

When two verbs are used together, the second one often is an infinitive (e.g., *to do*) or an *-ing* (e.g., *doing*) form.	
Some verbs take only infinitives. For example, *agree, decide, hope, manage, plan, promise,* and *wish*	They **promised to buy** her a book.
Some verbs take only *-ing* forms. For example, *avoid, delay, dislike, discuss, enjoy, finish,* and *(don't) mind*	We **enjoy staying** here each year.
Some verbs can take either infinitives or *-ing* forms with almost no difference in meaning. For example, *continue, hate, like, love,* and *prefer*	I **prefer eating** at home, but my partner **prefers going out**.

D 🎧 7 Listen to some parents talk about their children. Check (✓) whether each parent uses an infinitive or an *-ing* form after the verb. Then listen again and practice saying what you hear.

1. ☐ infinitive ☐ *-ing* form   4. ☐ infinitive ☐ *-ing* form
2. ☐ infinitive ☐ *-ing* form   5. ☐ infinitive ☐ *-ing* form
3. ☐ infinitive ☐ *-ing* form   6. ☐ infinitive ☐ *-ing* form

✓ **GOAL CHECK** Express Degrees of Liking

Complete the tasks.

1. In pairs, put these expressions in order from most like to most dislike: *be mad about, like, dislike, don't mind, can't stand*. Then, discuss whether an infinitive, an *-ing* form, or both can come after each expression.

   _____ _____ _____ _____ _____

2. Work on your own. Use each expression in a sentence about your own likes and dislikes.

3. Interview your classmates to find someone who: **Name**

   • can't stand something you like.   _____

   • likes something that you dislike.   _____

   • doesn't mind something that you dislike.   _____

   • is mad about something you don't mind.   _____

GOAL Discuss Mental Influences

Listening

A Look at the girls in the photo. What similarities and differences do you think they have? For example, do you think one might be more polite or outgoing than the other? Discuss in a group.

> I think the mother should pay attention to her child.

> I agree! I might tell her to put down her phone.

B Read these situations in pairs. Discuss what you think about each person's actions, and what you might say to him or her.

- You are at a park. A young boy is crying. A woman sitting next to the boy is looking at her phone instead of taking care of him.

- You are at a drugstore. You have been waiting to pay for a long time. Suddenly, a man runs to the front of the line. He buys one thing and leaves the store without saying sorry to anyone.

C 🎧 8 Listen to an interview and take notes. Then, choose the right answers.

1. What do the speakers say about cognitive biases?

   a. They change how people talk to each other.

   b. They affect how people understand things.

Cognitive bias can make it hard to believe the truth about Lucy and Maria Aylmer: they are twins!

2. What is an example of the halo effect?

    a. Believing that somebody wearing great clothes is probably also very intelligent

    b. Preferring to spend time with, and talk to, people who are attractive and nice

3. What is an example of the actor-observer bias?

    a. A boy who tells some people he failed a test because he was sick on the test day, but tells other people he failed because he did not study enough.

    b. A girl who believes that she failed a test because she was sick on the test day, but believes other people failed because they did not study enough.

To **influence** someone or something means to affect the person or thing.

D Work in a group. Discuss these questions.

1. Do you think the halo effect might have influenced your answers to **A**? Why?

2. Do you think actor-observer bias could have influenced your answers to **B**? Why?

3. What are some positive reasons why the people in **B** might have acted in those ways?

PRONUNCIATION: *th* Sounds

The letters *th* may be voiced (which means your throat vibrates) or unvoiced (no vibration).

voiced (/ð/)	**unvoiced** (/θ/)
the, that, breathe	*thin, both, theater*

In names, *th* is sometimes pronounced as /t/, such as in *Thomas* or *River Thames*.
In some compound words, *th* is pronounced separately as /t/ and then /h/, such as in *adulthood*.

E 🎧 9   Look at the phrases from the interview. Say the **bold** words with voiced and unvoiced *th* sounds and check (✓) the correct pronunciation. Then, listen to check your answers.

1. products **they're** advertising   ☐ voiced   ☐ unvoiced

2. to buy **those** products   ☐ voiced   ☐ unvoiced

3. makes us **think** they are   ☐ voiced   ☐ unvoiced

4. Here's **another** cognitive   ☐ voiced   ☐ unvoiced

5. a mother **with** her son   ☐ voiced   ☐ unvoiced

6. the **mother** looks angry   ☐ voiced   ☐ unvoiced

✓ **GOAL CHECK** Discuss Mental Influences

In small groups, describe a time when your actions or the actions of somebody you know might have been affected by the halo effect or by actor-observer bias.

The Mind's Eye   **21**

GOAL Talk about Personal Characteristics

Language Expansion: Personality Characteristics

WORD FOCUS

A person's **attitude** is how he or she behaves or thinks.

A Complete the definitions of these words to describe people's personalities with the correct form of the verb in parentheses: infinitive, *-ing* form, or some other form.

1. An anxious person may _____ (worry) a lot about things in his life.

2. Cheerful people usually _____ (have) a positive attitude, not a negative one.

3. Easygoing people usually stay calm and avoid _____ (get) upset.

4. People who are outgoing enjoy _____ (spend) time with others.

5. Reliable people usually want _____ (do) what other people expect.

6. A man who is selfish _____ (think) about himself, not other people.

7. A sensible person usually _____ (make) non-emotional decisions.

8. Those who are shy usually don't like _____ (meet) new people.

B In small groups, make a list of other words to describe people's personal characteristics. Share your list with the class.

C **MY WORLD** Work in a small group. Share some words that describe your personality or the personality of a person you know well.

Matias is my brother. He is really extroverted.

Yes, he loves talking to people.

Tourists take a photo in Chonqing, China.

Grammar

Using *Could*, *May*, and *Might*

Could, *may*, and *might* are modals. We use them before a base verb (e.g., *could* + *be*).

Use these modals to show that you are uncertain something is true.	Ed isn't here. He **might** be sick. Or he **could** have other plans.
Use these modals to say something is possible now or in the future.	Sue **may** take a vacation soon. She **could** go to Lima, Peru.

D 🎧 10 Listen to the conversation. Write the word you hear in each blank: *could, may*, or *might*. Then, in pairs, practice the conversation. Finally, make five changes to the conversation and practice again.

Ellen: I'm not getting along with my roommate. I (1) _____ move out.

Ali: Really? Why? Your roommate seems very nice to me.

Ellen: For one thing, she's not easygoing. My friends came over last night, and she asked us to make less noise.

Ali: Well, exams are coming up soon. She (2) _____ have wanted to study.

Ellen: You (3) _____ be right ... but still, every time I invite her out, she says "no." Doesn't that seem kind of rude?

Ali: Not really. She (4) _____ just be shy and introverted rather than outgoing like you.

Ellen: Maybe ... You know what? I (5) _____ talk to her this evening and find out more about her personality.

Ali: I think that's a good idea.

SPEAKING STRATEGY

Giving reasons
For one thing,...
On top of that,...
You might be right, but still...

E Complete the tasks in small groups.

1. Look at the photo on the previous page. Discuss which words from **A** and **B** might describe the women in the photo.

2. Share your ideas with another group. Did you use the same words to describe the people?

> The woman in the black blouse might be extroverted.

> She could be confident, too!

✓ GOAL CHECK Talk about Personal Characteristics

Make three lists of words to describe the characteristics you want in a close friend, a teacher, and a manager. Then, complete the steps.

1. In pairs, take turns sharing the words from one of your lists, but don't say which list it is. Can your partner guess which person you are describing?

2. Repeat step 1 twice more, with a different partner each time, until you have shared all three lists.

GOAL Discuss Improving Your Memory

Reading

A Complete the tasks in small groups.

1. Write two titles: *Physical Activities* and *Mental Activities*.

2. Add these activities to one or both lists: swimming, climbing, chess, video games.

3. Add five more activities to each list.

4. Join another group. Read your lists aloud once.

5. Try to write the other group's lists from your memory.

B Skim the article. Which of these titles is the best alternative? Why? Discuss in pairs.

a. People at the World Memory Championship

b. Cicero's Memory Method from Ancient Rome

c. Memory Competitions and Memory Methods

C Read the article and correct the errors.

1. The Mind Sports Olympiad is well known like the Olympic Games.

2. Yanjaa Wintersoul was born in Sweden but grew up in Mongolia.

3. Munkhshur Narmandakh set two world records.

4. Cicero wrote about the memory journey method over 1,000 years ago.

5. The memory journey method links ideas to people.

D Complete the steps in pairs.

1. Write a list of six items you want to buy. Do not show the list to your partner.

2. Listen to your partner's list. Use the memory journey method to remember the items.

3. Share your partner's list with the class. Your partner will say if you made any mistakes. Also share the ideas you "saw" in your mind to remember the items. Who had the funniest ideas? Was this method better than the one you used in **A**?

✓ GOAL CHECK

Discuss these questions as a class or in a group.

1. Do you think the memory journey method is useful? Why?

2. What other methods for improving your memory do you know? How useful are they?

How Memories Are Made

These days, there are many sports competitions that are a physical challenge to the athletes. Well-known and popular examples include the soccer World Cup and the summer and winter Olympic Games. There are other events, however, that are less well known, but also very challenging. Examples include the Mind Sports Olympiad, the Memoriad, and the World Memory Championships. These events are not physical competitions, but mental ones. At the World Memory Championships, for example, competitors have to **memorize** people's names and faces, **random** images, or **playing cards**.

The people who win gold at these events are very good at using their minds and their memory. Yanjaa Wintersoul is a memory athlete who was born in Mongolia but grew up in Sweden. At an international memory competition in Indonesia in 2017, Yanjaa achieved two world records. One for remembering 212 names and faces in 15 minutes, and one for remembering 354 images in five minutes. At a different event in 2017, Munkhshur Narmandakh, another woman from Mongolia, not only became the memory world champion, but also set a world record by remembering 1,924 playing cards in one hour.

Yanjaa and Munkhshur definitely have amazing mental abilities, but anybody can improve their memory. One method for developing a better memory has been known for a long time: A famous Roman named Cicero wrote about it more than 2,000 years ago. This method has many names, including the "memory journey." The **process** is simple. First, think about a familiar place or journey, such as the rooms in your home or your daily walk to work. Next, think of some items to remember and connect each item in your mind to one room in the place, or one location on the journey. Funny, crazy, or interesting connections are best because they are easier to remember. Finally, to remember the items, "walk" the journey in your mind and "see" the items in each location.

Imagine you need to remember a shopping list. You might connect each item to the rooms in your home. For example, you might imagine seeing some bananas "sleeping" in your bed. You could also imagine opening a bedroom door made of bread and watching some eggs rolling down your stairs. Finally, you might imagine swimming across a river of orange juice outside your front door. Then, when you go shopping, you "walk" from your bedroom to your front door in your mind and "see" what you need to buy: bananas, bread, eggs, and orange juice.

memorize to learn something so you remember it perfectly
random happening without any regular pattern and without anybody choosing or deciding it
playing cards used for playing games; they have numbers, pictures, and symbols on them
process a series of steps or events for doing something that happens in a specific order

GOAL Describe an Emotional Experience

Communication

A In small groups, match these emotions to the correct pictures. Then, discuss some situations in which people might experience each emotion.

anger	disgust
fear	happiness
sadness	surprise

_____

_____

_____

_____

disgust

_____

_____

B Interview some of your classmates to complete the table.

1. How many people have been angry more often than you this week?	
2. Who cannot remember the last time he or she was disgusted?	
3. Who has recently seen something that made him or her feel fear?	
4. How many people have felt both happiness and sadness this week?	
5. Who really loves being surprised by something? Who really hates it?	

Writing

C Read this paragraph about an emotional experience. Then work in pairs to match each underlined phrase to the unasked question that it answers.

On my birthday <u>two years ago</u>, <u>my family and friends</u> did not give me any gifts or even say "Happy birthday!" <u>This made me feel very sad</u>, of course. <u>In the evening</u>, I texted some friends <u>to see if they wanted to go out</u>, but they all said they were too busy. <u>This made me kind of angry</u>. Then somebody knocked on my door. When I opened it, <u>my family and all of my friends were standing there</u>! They had come <u>to have a party</u> <u>at my home</u>. <u>I was very surprised, but also really happy</u> that people had not forgotten my birthday.

When
Who

D Complete the steps.

1. Work on your own. Plan and then write one paragraph about a time when you experienced one or more emotions. Make sure you answer some unasked questions your readers might have. Use the paragraph in **C** as a guide.

2. Share your first draft with a partner. Take turns giving each other feedback.

3. Work on your own. Use your partner's feedback to write a better second draft. Then submit it to your teacher.

✓ GOAL CHECK Describe an Emotional Experience

Talk about a positive emotional experience you had recently. Say:

- What the experience was
- Where and when you had it
- Who was with you when you had it
- And how it made you feel

Take one minute to prepare, and then speak for 1–2 minutes.

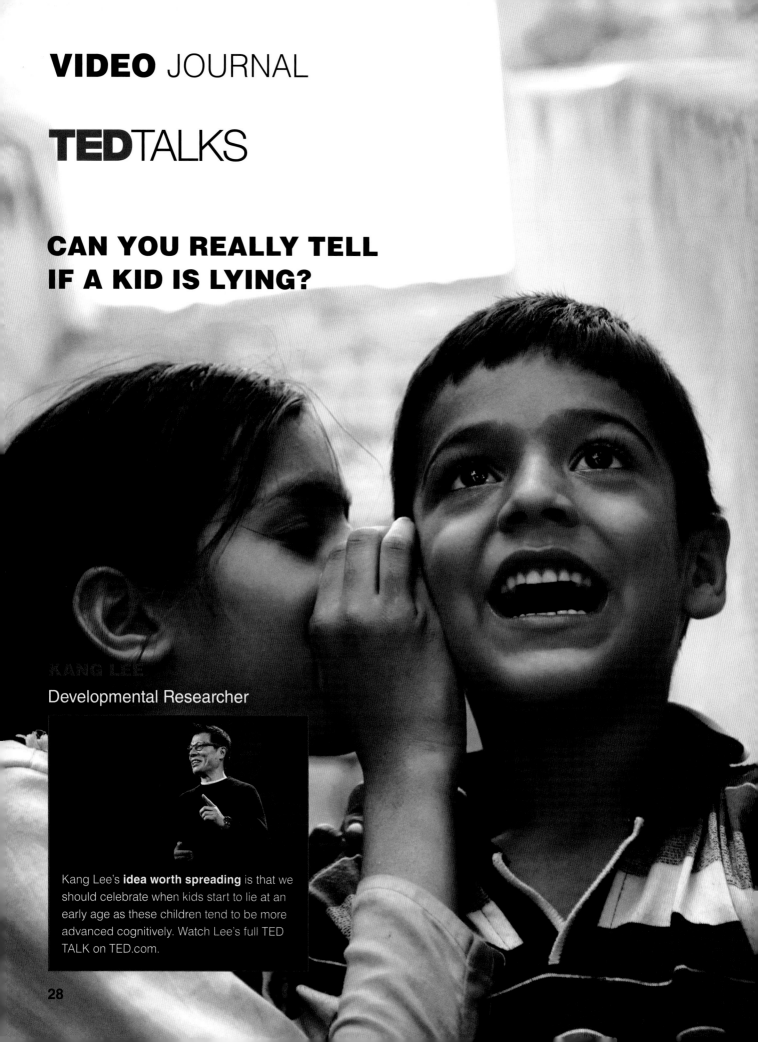

VIDEO JOURNAL

TEDTALKS

CAN YOU REALLY TELL IF A KID IS LYING?

KANG LEE

Developmental Researcher

Kang Lee's **idea worth spreading** is that we should celebrate when kids start to lie at an early age as these children tend to be more advanced cognitively. Watch Lee's full TED TALK on TED.com.

A Read the **idea worth spreading** from Kang Lee's talk. In small groups, discuss what you think it means.

B Work in a different group. Discuss the advantages of watching TED Talks by people like Kang Lee.

C Watch the first part of the talk. As you watch, underline the correct answer in each statement.

1. People generally believe *two / three* common things about children and lying.

2. One common belief is that children start lying *before / after* they start elementary school.

3. *Some / All* of the common beliefs people have about children and lying are wrong.

4. About *13 / 30* percent of children who are two years old will tell lies.

5. Among children who are four years old, more than 80 percent tell *the truth / lies*.

D Watch the second part of the talk. Discuss which child told a lie, and why.

E Watch the final part of the talk. CIrcle **T** for *true* or **F** for *false*. In pairs, discuss how to change the false statements to make them true.

1. Judges are good at knowing when children tell lies, but police officers are not.   **T**   **F**

2. Most parents are good at recognizing when their own children tell lies.   **T**   **F**

3. When children lie, they usually have a neutral expression on their faces.   **T**   **F**

4. The blood under the skin on people's faces can show their emotions and lies.   **T**   **F**

5. In the future, Kang Lee's discovery might be helpful for teachers or doctors.   **T**   **F**

F In pairs, discuss whether Lee would probably agree (*A*) or disagree (*D*) with each statement, and why.

- Telling lies is a natural part of development for all children.   A   D

- Some groups of people are good at recognizing children's lies.   A   D

- In general, children are not very good at telling believable lies.   A   D

- The discovery of transdermal optical imaging will benefit society.   A   D

G Lee explains how transdermal optical imaging technology might be good for teachers. In small groups, discuss how it might be good or bad for these people.

> parents
>
> police officers
>
> politicians
>
> students

H **MY WORLD** Discuss these questions in a small group. Be honest!

1. When and why did you or your siblings tell lies when you were a child?

2. Were your parents or other adults good at knowing when you were lying?

I Work in a different small group. Discuss these questions.

1. Every human tells lies sometimes. Why do you think this is true?

2. Because of Lee's discovery of transdermal optical imaging, it may be impossible in the future for people to tell lies that other people believe. Do you think this is a good thing? Why?

Changing Planet

These days, animals must deal with the effects of humans on the environment. This hermit crab, for example, is using a piece of trash as a shell.

Look at the photo and answer the questions:

1 What do you see in the photo?

2 In what other ways have animals had to change because of humans?

UNIT 3 GOALS

A. Discuss Pollution

B. Discuss Causes and Effects

C. Discuss Animal Populations

D. Consider the Effects of Climate Change

E. Summarize Your Ideas

GOAL Discuss Pollution

Vocabulary

A Read the text. Does your town or city have a pollution problem? Discuss in pairs.

Tower Bridge, a famous landmark in London, UK, is barely visible through the fog on the River Thames.

In early December 1952, the weather in London was very cold. In their houses, people lit fires to stay warm. On the streets, they took cars, buses, or trains to work. There was little wind, so the cold air stayed over the city. Pollution from the fires and vehicles also stayed in the air. When people woke up on the morning of December 5th, they saw thick fog.

Londoners had experienced thick fogs for hundreds of years. These thick fogs were called *pea-soupers* because their color was like soup made from yellow peas. But the Great Smog of 1952 was the worst one ever. It was so thick and so dark that drivers could not see the lights of other cars, people walked into each other on the streets, and nobody could see the sun.

By Tuesday, December 9th, the fog was gone, but its effects continued. The air quality had been so bad that thousands of people died and about 100,000 became sick. Luckily, not all of the effects were negative. Soon after the Great Smog, the government created the Clean Air Act. This law helped people breathe easier by reducing the level of pollution across the country.

B Complete each definition with a blue word.

1. _____Quality_____ describes how good or bad something is.

2. A _____ is a rule that people in a country must follow.

3. A _____ situation is one that is bad or that has a bad effect.

4. A person who _____ something made it happen or exist.

5. If a person _____ something, it happened to him or her.

6. If dust, smoke, or fog is _____, it is hard to see through it.

7. People use _____ to travel from one place to another.

8. Something that makes air or water dirty is called _____.

9. The _____ of an action are what happens as a result of it.

10. The _____ of something like pollution is how much of it there is.

WORD FOCUS

Words that are commonly used together are called **collocations**.

C Complete each collocation below with a blue word from the article.

1. water or air _____

2. pollution _____

3. a _____ effect

4. _____ fog or clouds

Grammar

The Passive 1

The passive (or passive voice) is formed using *be* + past participle of the main verb.	Pollution **is caused** by vehicles. People **are affected** by pollution.
To turn an active sentence into a passive one, the direct object of the active verb becomes the subject of the passive verb. (For this reason, verbs that do not take a direct object usually cannot be passive.) You can add the subject of the active verb to the passive sentence after *by* as the agent.	Pollution causes many problems. <small>subject active verb direct object</small> Many problems are caused by pollution. <small>subject passive verb agent</small>

The passive is more common in formal, written English than in informal, spoken English. The passive is used:
1. to emphasize the object of a verb by making it the subject of the passive sentence.
2. when the agent (the person or thing doing the action) is unknown, unimportant, or obvious.

D Read the beginning of a conversation. Which speaker uses a passive?

Carlos: I didn't know that London used to have bad pollution. Did you?
Sofia: Actually, yes. I was told about the Great Smog by a friend.
Carlos: Was he living there when it happened?
Sofia: No way! He's the same age as us!

E 🎧 12 Read the rest of the conversation. Circle the correct answers. Then listen to check your answers.

Carlos: Have you ever experienced bad pollution?
Sofia: There was a lot of pollution in my city last year. A law
(1) *passed / was passed* by the government, and people (2) *told / were told* not to drive their cars for a week.
Carlos: Wow. What (3) *happened / was happened*?
Sofia: The law (4) *worked / was worked*. The level of pollution
(5) *reduced / was reduced* a lot.
Carlos: Good. I bet many people were unhappy about not driving, though.

F Complete each definition with a word from the box. One word is extra.

1. Water pollution means the water in an area is not _____.
2. If a place has smog or the air is _____, it has air pollution.
3. A place with a noise pollution problem can be very _____.
4. Places that are never _____ have a light pollution problem.

clean
dark
dusty
loud
strong

 GOAL CHECK Discuss Pollution

Tell your classmates which kind of pollution is the biggest problem where you live: water, air, noise, or light. Say what the pollution is caused by and explain why it is a problem.

GOAL   Discuss Causes and Effects

Listening

A You will hear an interview with a scientist discussing "extreme weather events." In pairs, discuss what you think this expression means.

B 🎧 13 Listen to the first part of the interview. Check your ideas from **A**. Then number the types of extreme weather discussed in the order you hear them.

Flood

Heatwave

Snowstorm

Tornado

C 🎧 14 Listen to the second part of the interview. Complete each statement with two words that the scientist says.

1. A few extreme weather events happen _____.
2. Extreme weather events are becoming _____.
3. News stories often discuss big floods or _____.
4. Extreme weather is probably happening more because of _____.
5. To fix the problem, humans need to produce _____.

A levee is a natural or man-made wall which holds back flood water. This man-made levee protects a home in Vicksburg, Mississippi.

PRONUNCIATION: Linking Words Together

Whether two words are linked together in speech depends on the sound at the end of the first word and the beginning of the second.

consonant sound → same sound	link	***heavier rain → heavie‿rain***
consonant sound → a/e/i/o/u sound	link	***the reason is → the reaso‿nis***
a/e/i sound → a/e/i/o/u sound	link with *y* sound	***agree on → agree‿yon***
o/u sound → a/e/i/o/u sound	link with *w* sound	***and so on → and so‿won***

D 🎧 **15** Read the extract from the interview. Underline the words that should be linked together. Then listen to check your answers.

Why are extreme weather events happening more? The most likely reason is

climate change. A hotter climate leads to warmer summers, but also heavier rain,

colder winters, more storms, and so on. How can we fix it? One way would be

to produce clean energy.

E In pairs, take turns reading the extract in **D** aloud. Make sure you link the words together.

Communication

F Answer the questions in your notebook. Then interview two students and write down their answers. Finally, work in pairs and share what you learned.

1. What is one thing that causes pollution?

2. What is one effect of pollution?

3. What is one cause of climate change?

4. What is one negative effect of extreme weather events?

SPEAKING STRATEGY

Explaining cause and effect
One cause of this is ...
This was caused by ...
As a result, ...
This led to ...

G Complete the chart with a global situation, or a personal situation. Add causes and effects.

Situation:	→	Cause(s):	→	Effect(s):

 GOAL CHECK
Discuss Causes and Effects

In small groups, take turns sharing the cause(s) and effect(s) of your situation, but don't say what your situation is. The other group members will listen and try to guess the situation.

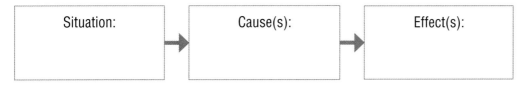

This situation is making me really tired and stressed. I'm studying until late every day and not seeing my friends.

Are you preparing for an exam?

C GOAL Discuss Animal Populations

Language Expansion: Saying large numbers

hundreds (100s)	524 → five hundred (and) twenty-four
thousands (1,000s)	1,250 → one thousand, two hundred (and) fifty
ten thousands (10,000s)	17,400 → seventeen thousand, (and) four hundred
hundred thousands (100,000s)	432,060 → four hundred thirty-two thousand, (and) sixty
millions (1,000,000s)	2,400,900 → two million, four hundred thousand, (and) nine hundred

A Complete the article on climate change with the numbers from the box. Then compare answers in pairs.

400
45,000
200,000
350,000
127,000,000

When we talk about climate change, we often focus on how it affects humans. However, it affects every species on the planet. Saiga antelope, an endangered species, were affected by the effects of climate change in 2015. Around (1) _____ of the animals died over a period of two weeks. This was about 60 percent of a population of roughly (2) _____ saiga. Scientists believed the deaths had been caused by bacteria. These bacteria, normally not dangerous to saiga, can poison the animals when the weather becomes hotter and more humid.

Another example happened in Australia in the summer of 2014. The temperature had climbed to 105 degrees Fahrenheit. It was so hot that thousands of flying foxes, a kind of bat, died. It is estimated that at least (3) _____ of these bats were killed by the heat in a single day. Events like this continue to happen. Early in 2018, a smaller number of flying foxes—about (4) _____—were found dead near Sydney.

The effects of climate change are not always bad for animals. For example, the population of Japan is about (5) _____, but people are moving away from the countryside and small villages to big cities. This means there are fewer people to control wild pigs called boars. In addition, warmer weather means farmers can grow more food. Boars are visiting their farms to eat the food, which is creating big problems for farmers.

Critically endangered Saiga antelope in a nature reserve in Kalmykia, Russia

Grammar

The Past Perfect	
Use the past perfect to talk about something that happened before another event in the past. subject + *had* + *(not)* + past participle	Local people discovered that hundreds of fruit bats **had died** because of the heat.
If the order in which things happened is clear or not important, either the past perfect or simple past can be used. Often, a word like *before* or *after* is added so the order is clear.	The bacteria **had not been** dangerous before the heat and humidity got worse. The bacteria **were not** dangerous before the heat and humidity got worse.

B In pairs, underline examples of the past perfect in the text on the previous page.

C Read each sentence and underline the event that happened first. Then rewrite the sentences in your notebook so the event is in the past perfect.

1. The Great Smog of 1952 made about 100,000 people sick before it ended.
2. After the smog ended, the government passed a law to clean up the air.
3. Approximately 200,000 antelope died because the weather became hotter.
4. Human populations decreased, so wild boars became a problem.

Conversation

D 🎧 16 Close your book and listen to the conversation. Who saw a wild boar?

Kenzo: Look at this photo, Paula. It was taken by my grandma.
Paula: That's not a pig, is it, Kenzo?
Kenzo: No, it's a wild boar. It was standing outside her front door one day.
Paula: Wow! What did she do?
Kenzo: She called the police, but by the time they arrived, the boar had gone.
Paula: That sounds so scary. I'm glad it didn't happen to me!

SPEAKING STRATEGY

Expressing Surprise
Wow!
That's not a pig, is it?
I can't believe it!

E Practice the conversation in pairs. Then add some details and events to make it more funny or interesting. Share it with the class.

F Talk about a funny or interesting event that happened to you recently. Use the past perfect.

 GOAL CHECK Discuss Animal Populations

Choose one of the endangered species below or find one of your own. Research the answers to the questions. Then share what you learned in groups.

Animals
California condors
Bengal tigers
Galápagos penguin
_____

Questions
- What was the animal's population in the past?
- What is its current population?
- How has it been affected by climate change or human activities?
- What could humans do to keep it safe in the future?

D GOAL Consider the Effects of Climate Change

A In pairs, read the title of the text. How do you feel about the idea that coffee might be in danger? Why?

B In new pairs, discuss which numbers about coffee are correct and circle them. Then scan the first paragraph of the text to confirm your answers.

1. The amount of land on which coffee is grown (in acres):
   270,000 / 27 million

2. The amount spent on coffee by US businesses (in dollars):
   5.5 million / 5.5 billion

3. The money made by US businesses from coffee (in dollars):
   12 billion / 12 trillion

4. The number of cups of coffee drunk by people each year:
   500 million / 500 billion

5. The number of people who work on farms growing coffee:
   25 million / 250 million

6. The weight of coffee grown each year (in school buses):
   380,000 / 830,000

C Read the text and look at these statements. Write *T* for *true*, *F* for *false*, or *NG* if there is no information about it in the text.

_____ 1. Coffee is grown in one quarter of the world's countries.

_____ 2. No other country grows more coffee each year than Brazil.

_____ 3. Coffee plants can die if they get too much rain.

_____ 4. Farmers in Brazil plan to grow new plants before 2050.

_____ 5. Coffee berry borer beetles make coffee plants sick.

_____ 6. Coffee berry borer beetles cause millions in damage yearly.

✓ GOAL CHECK

Work in pairs. Which of these statements are supported by the text. Then discuss how climate change is affecting your life as well.

a. Climate change could soon affect a huge, global industry.

b. Climate change could affect everything from bugs to plants, to people, to society.

c. Climate change must be combatted by people working together.

d. Climate change may help people living in some regions or doing some jobs.

Is Coffee in Danger?

Around the world, coffee is grown in dozens of countries by 25 million farmworkers on about 27 million acres of land. That's more than seven percent of the Earth's surface! Just in Brazil, the world's largest coffee grower, almost 6.2 billion pounds of coffee are grown each year. That's the same weight as about 380,000 school buses. The world needs this much coffee because every year, people drink more than 500 billion cups. Businesses in the United States spend about $5.5 billion to bring coffee into the country, and make more than $12 billion by selling it. In other words, coffee is big business.

Unfortunately, climate change could be a big threat to this business and the people who depend on it. To grow good coffee, the weather must be just right. If it is too hot or too cold, or if there is too much or too little rain, the plants might die or the coffee beans might be poor quality. Climate change is making the world hotter and changing where and how much rain falls. This means many regions that have perfect weather for growing coffee now will not be good places to grow coffee in the future. In Brazil, for example, scientists say that more than half of good coffee land will not be usable by the year 2050.

Even worse for coffee, an insect called the coffee berry borer beetle that likes to eat coffee beans also loves hotter weather. This means that as the climate changes, there will be more of these insects living in more places. And if there are more coffee berry borers, more coffee plants will be attacked. They already cause $500 million in damage each year; how much will they cause in the future? In addition, diseases such as coffee rust (a disease that causes the tree to lose its ability to produce berries/beans) become more common when the weather is hotter and wetter. In Central America in 2011, this disease began to spread from coffee farm to coffee farm. In total, it affected more than half of the land that was used for growing coffee, and 350,000 people lost their jobs.

Coffee is the favorite drink of people all over the world. But unless humans work together to stop climate change and protect coffee, it could become part of our history, not our future.

GOAL Summarize Your Ideas

Writing

> **WRITING SKILL:** Writing a Summary
>
> Writing a summary of information you have read or heard is a valuable skill. In general, a good summary should:
>
> - be shorter than the original and include only main points and details, not minor ideas or examples. Note that the points and details you include do not have to be in the same order as in the original.
>
> - mostly be written in your own words, paraphrasing the original rather than copying or quoting it.
>
> - be accurate; don't change or add information that was not in the original.

A Compare this summary of the Great Smog of London with the text on page 32. Several problem areas are underlined. Work with a partner to decide what each problem is and then rewrite the underlined parts.

In December, 1952, the air in London was polluted by fires and traffic. There was no wind, so the pollution caused a thick fog called a *pea-souper*. People in London had experienced thick fogs like this for centuries. The fog was so thick that people could not see the lights of cars or even the sun. The fog probably smelled bad, too. After a few days, the fog went away, but its effects continued. Many people became sick, and thousands died. As a result of this bad fog, the British government passed a law that reduced the level of pollution across the country.

B Choose a source from this unit. Then write a summary of it in your notebook. Follow these steps when you write your summary.

Step 1: Choose your source: the interview about extreme weather events, the reading about how climate change affects animals, or the reading about the effects of climate change on coffee.

Step 2: Read or listen to your source again and take notes.

Step 3: Write an outline of your summary using your notes to help you.

Step 4: Write a draft summary.

Step 5: Review and revise your draft. Make sure your summary includes only major ideas, uses your own words, and does not change anything or add any new information.

Communication

 Slogans are short, powerful phrases that are easy to remember and that help people understand and spread an important message. In small groups, discuss what these climate change-related slogans mean. Then rank them in order from the most powerful message to the least powerful.

_____ Climate change: *It's really not cool.*

_____ Climate change: *There is no planet B.*

_____ Climate change: *You can't just open a window.*

_____ Climate change: *It's not the end of the world. Probably.*

You must be the change you wish to see in the world.

✓ GOAL CHECK
Summarize Your Ideas

Gandhi believed that people need to make changes in their own lives in order to change the world. In pairs, complete these steps.

Step 1: Decide on a change you will easily make in your own lives that will help the environment. If possible, decide on a change that other people could also make.

Step 2: Prepare a 60-second talk about the change you will make. Your talk should mention the change you will make, how it will benefit the environment, and how people can do it.

Step 3: Come up with a slogan you can mention during or at the end of your talk to help people understand and remember your idea.

Step 4: Practice giving your talk. Make sure you both speak.

Step 5: Join another pair of students. Take turns delivering your talks.

VIDEO JOURNAL

TEDTALKS

TALES OF ICE-BOUND WONDERLANDS

PAUL NICKLEN

National Geographic
Photographer; Biologist

Paul Nicklen's **idea worth spreading** is
that the loss of polar ice could devastate
entire ecosystems, including the remarkable
animals that inhabit them. Watch Nicklen's
full TED Talk on TED.com.

A Check (✓) the statement that is closest
in meaning to Paul Nicklen's **idea worth
spreading**. (If necessary, use a dictionary to
check any words you don't know in Nicklen's
Idea.)

☐ **a.** If ice in the Arctic and Antarctic melts,
many species could be badly affected.

☐ **b.** Many kinds of animals can live in cold
areas that have a lot of ice and snow.

☐ **c.** When there is not enough polar ice,
it can have a big effect on climate
change.

B In his TED Talk, Nicklen says that leopard seals have "a bad reputation," which means that people have a negative opinion about them. Discuss these questions in a small group.

1. Look at the picture. Why do you think leopard seals might have a bad reputation?

2. What other animals have a bad reputation? Do they deserve this reputation? Why?

3. Think of an animal. If the animal could talk, what reputation would it say humans have? Why?

C In small groups, predict which of these adjectives will describe Nicklen's TED Talk about his adventures in Antarctica. Then watch the TED Talk and confirm your predictions.

educational	exciting	funny
negative	serious	worrying

D In pairs, discuss whether Nicklen would probably agree (*A*) or disagree (*D*) with each idea. If you think he would disagree, how could you change the idea so he would agree?

1. It is more important for children to use technology than to play outside.

2. If Arctic summer ice is lost, humans will have lost something important.

3. The female leopard seal tried to help him in several different ways.

4. In general, leopard seals do not deserve to have a bad reputation.

5. The things that humans do are a danger to animals like leopard seals.

E Work with a different partner. Take turns sharing the adjectives you predicted would describe Nicklen's talk. Then discuss the three best adjectives that actually do describe his talk.

Teenage workers playing
in a textile factory in
Rajasthan, India

UNIT 4 GOALS

A. Talk about the Things You Value

B. Discuss Important People or Events

C. Discuss Good Financial Habits

D. Talk about Great Jobs

E. Express Agreement or Disagreement

45

A GOAL Talk about the Things You Value

Vocabulary

A Read the text. In pairs, discuss its main idea.

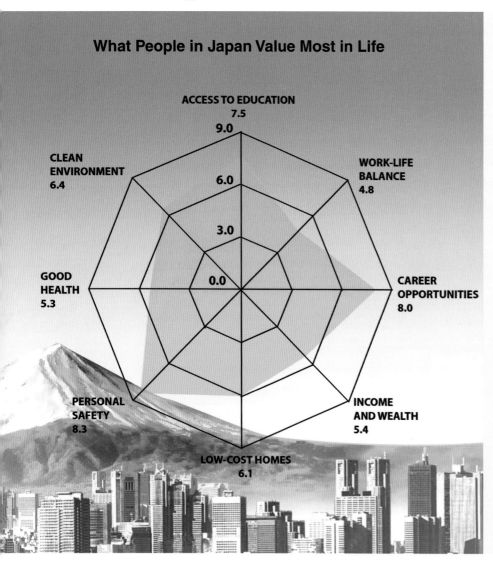

What People in Japan Value Most in Life

ACCESS TO EDUCATION
7.5

WORK-LIFE BALANCE
4.8

CLEAN ENVIRONMENT
6.4

CAREER OPPORTUNITIES
8.0

GOOD HEALTH
5.3

INCOME AND WEALTH
5.4

PERSONAL SAFETY
8.3

LOW-COST HOMES
6.1

To find out about the things that people value most in life, the Organisation for Economic Co-operation and Development (OECD) asked people in many countries. The OECD's questions asked people to give a score for several criteria, or topics, based on how good they felt about these parts of their lives. The average score for all topics is the overall level of life satisfaction in that country. The criteria were: having access to high-quality education; being able to find a balance between work and other parts of life; having good opportunities for a successful career; making a good income and having enough wealth; being able to afford a nice home; feeling safe; having good health and access to high-quality medical care; and living in a clean environment.

B Complete each definition with a word in blue from the text.

1. _____ are situations that give you the possibility to do something.

2. _____ are the things you think about when you judge something.

3. _____ is how much money or valuable goods a person has.

4. A _____ is your job or the work you do during your working life.

5. To _____ something means having enough money to buy it.

6. To _____ something means to think that it is very important.

7. Having _____ to a thing means you have the right to use or see it.

8. Two things that are in _____ have the same weight or importance.

9. Your _____ is the money that you get from working or investing.

10. Your _____ with a thing is how happy and good you feel about it.

WORD FOCUS

Investing is the process of using money to try to make more money.

C Expand your vocabulary. Complete this table in pairs. Use a dictionary if necessary.

Noun	Verb	Adjective
balance	(1) _____	balanced
access	(2) _____	(3) _____
satisfaction	(4) _____	satisfied
(5) _____	afford	(6) _____
(7) _____	value	(8) _____

D **MY WORLD** In small groups, discuss these questions. Explain your answers.

1. What is more important: access to good education or to high-quality healthcare?

2. Some people say satisfaction comes from having wealth. Do you agree?

Grammar

Infinitives and *-ing* Forms 2	
Both infinitives and *-ing* forms can be the subject of a sentence.	**Finding out / To find out** the information is important.
Infinitives can give more information about some nouns and adjectives.	She doesn't have enough <u>time</u> **to do** it. It is <u>important</u> **to finish** it soon.
-ing forms can be the object of a preposition.	He is good <u>at</u> **doing** that.

E In pairs, find and underline examples of infinitives and *-ing* forms in **A**. Then in **B**, rewrite definitions 5 and 6 to start with an *-ing* form and definition 7 to start with an infinitive.

F Complete each sentence with the correct form of the word in parentheses.

1. I need _____ (save) money to afford a home.

2. _____ (stay) healthy is important.

3. She is interested in _____ (change) her career.

4. I need more opportunities _____ (learn).

✓ **GOAL CHECK** Talk about the Things You Value

1. Decide how much you value each of the eight criteria in the chart in **A**. Assign a score, from 8 points for the most important thing to 1 point for the least important one.

2. In a small group, calculate the average score for each criterion. Use the average score to create a chart like the one in **A**.

3. Compare your chart with other groups. How are they similar and different?

GOAL Discuss Important People or Events

A lollipop is a type of candy.

Listening

A Add an *-ing* phrase to complete this sentence about your life. For example, you might write *Coming to this country...* or *Going to school...*

_____ changed my life.

B In groups, share and discuss your sentences from **A**. Then, discuss these questions.

1. What is more likely to change people's lives: a person or a thing? Why?

2. What is more likely to improve people's lives: a small change or a big one? Why?

C 🎧 18 Listen to a conversation between two friends and take notes. Then put the events in the order they happened.

1. Josh tells a story about a man named Drew.

Josh's story

_____ **a.** Drew Dudley's actions and words changed the woman's life.

_____ **b.** The woman thought about leaving school and going home.

_____ **c.** The woman met Drew Dudley when he was giving out lollipops.

_____ **d.** The woman was worried about starting college.

2. Ian tells a story about something his teacher did.

Ian's story

_____ **a.** Ian's teacher wrote the message on the board.

_____ **b.** Other students were not nice to the new boy.

_____ **c.** The message made Ian change how he acted.

_____ **d.** The new boy became a student at Ian's school.

D Discuss these questions in small groups.

1. How could you explain the idea of a "lollipop moment" to someone who has never heard of it?

2. Is it always a good idea to thank people who did or said something that changed your life? Why?

Pronunciation: Saying *To*

In most cases, *to* has a short vowel sound (/tə/).	She decided **to** leave college. /tə/
In some common expressions, *to* links to the previous word and the /t/ sound is not pronounced.	She's **going to** stay with friends. /gənə/
When *to* begins or ends a sentence, or when the speaker wants to emphasize it, *to* has a long vowel sound (/tu/).	She said she doesn't know how **to**. /tu/

E 🎧 19 In pairs, take turns saying *to* with either a short or long vowel sound in these parts of the conversation from **C**. Check (✓) which pronunciation sounds best. Then listen and check your answers.

	short (/tə/)	long (/tu/)
1. a woman spoke *to* him one day	☐	☐
2. she wanted *to* go home, in fact	☐	☐
3. wanted people *to* donate money	☐	☐
4. it was dangerous *to* take candy	☐	☐
5. staying at college and decided *to*.	☐	☐

Communication

F In pairs, take turns asking and answering these questions.

1. What do you want to do over the weekend?
2. What is one thing you used to do a lot?
3. What is something you are going to do later?
4. Who is the last person you gave a gift to?

✓ GOAL CHECK Discuss Important People or Events

1. Complete the notes about an important person or event from your life.

   > Person / Event: _____
   > When it happened: _____
   > What happened: _____
   > How it changed you: _____
   > What you said to this person / what you would like to say / what you said to others about the event: _____

2. In small groups, take turns talking about the important person or event. When it is your turn to listen, take notes. Then use your notes to ask questions after the speaker has finished.

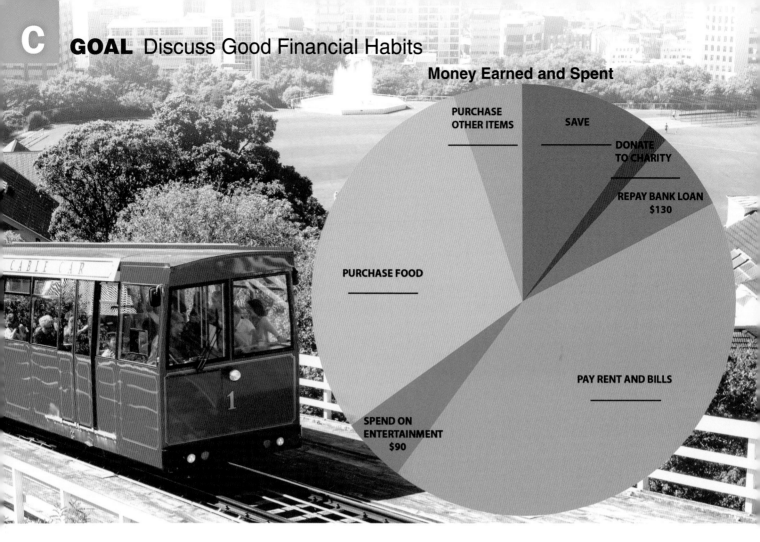

Money Earned and Spent

PURCHASE OTHER ITEMS _____

SAVE _____

DONATE TO CHARITY _____

REPAY BANK LOAN $130

PURCHASE FOOD _____

PAY RENT AND BILLS _____

SPEND ON ENTERTAINMENT $90

C GOAL Discuss Good Financial Habits

A
$30
$100
$200
$600
$850

B
buy
give
make
pay back
set aside

SPEAKING STRATEGY

Showing excitement
That's fantastic!
That's wonderful!
Congratulations!
Wow!

Language Expansion: Expressions Related to Money

A Together, David and Alessandra earn $2,000 each month. The pie chart shows what they do with their money. In pairs, complete the chart using the numbers in box A. Then match each word or phrase in box B to its synonym on the chart.

Conversation

B 🎧 20 In pairs, complete the conversation using words from box B. Then listen to check your answers.

Alessandra: David! I have great news! I was given a promotion today at work.

David: That's fantastic! Congratulations! You really deserve it.

Alessandra: Starting next month, I'm going to (1) _____ $500 more per month.

David: Wow! That's going to make a big difference in our lives.

Alessandra: I know. Should we invest it or (2) _____ our bank loan more quickly?

David: Let's repay our loan. And I think we should (3) _____ more money each month. I want us to (4) _____ a house so that we don't have to pay rent every month. The rent was raised a lot this year!

Alessandra: I agree. And if anything is left after our bills have all been paid, we could (5) _____ a little more money to charity, too.

50 Unit 4

C **MY WORLD** In small groups, take turns answering these questions:

1. Do you do the same things with your money as David and Alessandra?

2. How often do you do these things?

D In groups, imagine you will get an extra $500 each month. Discuss different things you could do with the money. What are the pros and cons of each idea?

WORD FOCUS

The **pros** and **cons** of something are its advantages and disadvantages.

Grammar

The Passive 2	
The passive is often used with simple verb forms.	He **is / 's given** the money every week. (simple present) He **was given** the money last week. (simple past) He **will / 'll be given** the money next week. (future) He **has / 's been given** the money this week. (present perfect)
The passive can also be used with continuous forms to talk about things that were, are, or will be in progress at a certain time.	He **is / 's being given** the money right now. (present continuous) He **was being given** the money yesterday at 11 a.m. (past continuous)

E In pairs, find and underline two examples of the passive in the conversation in **B**. Is each example present, past, present perfect, or future?

F Work with a different partner. Use the cues to write passive sentences. Use the information in the chart to help you.

1. the bills / pay (present perfect) _____

2. the money / donate to / charity (simple past) _____

3. the items / purchase / next week (future) _____

4. the bank loan / repay (past continuous) _____

5. the rent / pay / every month (simple present) _____

6. the food / buy / now (present continuous) _____

 GOAL CHECK Discuss Good Financial Habits

1. Write a list of three financial habits that can help you live a better life.

2. Share your list with a partner. Discuss the pros and cons of each habit and choose the best four.

3. Join another pair of students. Share your lists. Discuss the pros and cons of each habit and choose the best five.

4. Share your group's list with the class. After every group has shared their list, vote on the six best financial habits.

5. In your group, discuss which of the six habits you will start doing and why.

D GOAL Talk about Great Jobs

Reading

A In pairs, match the words to their definitions.

1. busy ____   **a.** causing a lot of worry
2. challenging ____   **b.** extremely tiring
3. depressing ____   **c.** hard or difficult
4. exhausting ____   **d.** having a lot to do
5. low-paid ____   **e.** making one feel sad
6. stressful ____   **f.** providing little money

B Read the text. Write **T** for *true* **F** for *false* or **NG** if the information is *not given* in the text.

____ **1.** People who do not feel life satisfaction may not take on challenges at work.

____ **2.** Dan Price raised his staff's salary to $75,000 a year.

____ **3.** Perpetual Guardian's plan was good for workers as well as for the company.

____ **4.** People who work at Airbnb can travel to another country for work or fun.

C In groups, discuss who you would most like to work for: Dan Price, Perpetual Guardian, or Airbnb? Why?

✓ GOAL CHECK

In pairs, imagine that you run a company and want to make a change to improve workers' lives.

1. Discuss the benefits of each option and choose one from each category.

2. Share your options and reasons with the class. Whose company offers the best benefits?

Pay benefits
get a salary of $75,000 a year / get a bonus when the company does well

Time benefits
work just four days a week / get eight weeks off a year / work from home once a week

Other perks
spend one morning a week on personal projects / get free gym membership / get free lunch at the office

Want a better job? Work for a better company

Some people love working so much that it doesn't feel like work. They wake up every day feeling excited about their careers. But most people are not so lucky. They need money to live, so they need a job. However, they don't love their work, and this can create problems. Because these workers are not satisfied with their jobs, they feel unhappy. And because they are unhappy, they may not work hard. Luckily, some people and companies are trying to improve things.

Dan Price is the CEO of a company based in Seattle. In 2015, he decided to pay the workers at his company more money. He raised the salaries of all of his workers to $70,000 a year, which is much higher than the US average income. To pay for this, he cut his own salary to the same amount. Interestingly, a study was published by Princeton University in 2010 about salaries. According to this research, people who make around $75,000 each year are happier and feel more satisfaction than those who make less or more money. Since Price made his decision, his workers have been happier and his company has been more successful.

Money is one reason why some workers are unhappy with their jobs. Another reason is working too many hours. Perpetual Guardian, a company based in New Zealand, wanted staff to have a better work-life balance. The company came up with a plan. Its staff were paid for five days, but they only had to work four days each week. Not surprisingly, workers were happier and more satisfied with their lives. They also worked harder, so the company was very pleased with the success of its plan.

Many studies about life satisfaction usually show that people who do things are happier than people who buy things. So, for example, going on a road trip or learning to play the guitar is better than buying a car or guitar. The famous company Airbnb wants its staff to have great experiences. Workers get $2,000 each year to stay at Airbnb properties anywhere in the world. In addition, workers have the opportunity to visit or work at offices in other countries. As a result, many people who work at Airbnb love their jobs.

GOAL Express Agreement or Disagreement

Communication

Communication Skill: Agreeing and Disagreeing

When speaking and writing, it is common to agree or disagree with a person or idea.		
Expressing agreement	I agree with (something) I agree that (idea)	I think / believe it's true that...
Expressing disagreement	I disagree with (something) I don't agree that (idea)	I think / believe that... is wrong (about)...
Expressing degrees of agreement	I completely agree that... I mostly disagree with...	I think you're partially right about...

WORD FOCUS

A **saying** is a well-known phrase about life that many people agree with.
Laughter is the thing you do and the sound you make when you laugh.

A In small groups, discuss what each saying means. Then use expressions from the box above to say how much you agree or disagree with each saying. Explain why.

1. The best things in life are free.

2. Laughter is the best medicine.

3. Good things come to those who wait.

4. You have to spend money to make money.

5. Good work isn't cheap; cheap work isn't good.

B Work in a different group. Complete these tasks.

1. Come up with a saying that you all agree with. Your saying could be one that is common in your country or one that you make up.

2. Share your saying with the class. Explain what it means and why you all agree with it.

3. How many other people in the class agree completely with your saying? Which group's saying was the most popular?

Students are studying at the University of Bahrain.

Writing

C In pairs, read the paragraph. Then answer the questions by writing sentence numbers in the spaces.

(1) A common saying is that "education can unlock any door." (2) In my opinion, this saying means that having a good education can help people do new things. (3) I mostly agree with this idea. (4) The reason is that I think education does give people more opportunities in life. (5) For example, my sister went to college for four years. Because of her good education, she was able to get a great job with a high salary. She also enjoys a good work-life balance. (6) However, my brother did not finish high school. Because he did not complete his education, he cannot find a good job. (7) So this is why I mostly agree that "education can unlock any door."

_____ **1.** Which sentence adds a concluding sentence?

_____ **2.** Which sentence explains the meaning of the saying?

_____ **3.** Which sentence gives a reason for a point of view?

_____ **4.** Which sentence gives an example to support an opinion?

_____ **5.** Which sentence includes a second, contrasting, example?

__1__ **6.** Which sentence introduces the saying to be discussed?

_____ **7.** Which sentence states the degree of agreement?

D Choose a saying from **A** and complete the paragraph in your own words.

A common saying is that _____

In my opinion, this saying means that _____

I _____ with this idea.

The reason is that _____

For example, _____

_____

However, _____

_____

So, this is why _____

_____

✓ GOAL CHECK Express Agreement or Disagreement

Choose one of the other sayings in **A** and write a paragraph to say how much you agree or disagree with it. 1. Use the paragraph on this page as a guide. 2. Share your writing with a partner. 3. Take turns helping each other find and fix mistakes. 4. Then, write and submit a second draft.

TEDTALKS

A LIFE LESSON FROM A VOLUNTEER FIREFIGHTER

MARK BEZOS

Head of Development, Robin Hood;
Volunteer Firefighter

Mark Bezos's **idea worth spreading** is that every act of generosity matters—even the small ones. Watch Bezos's full TED Talk on TED.com

A You will watch a TED Talk by Mark Bezos. Read the information. Then discuss the questions in pairs.

Mark Bezos is a busy man. He works in New York City at Robin Hood, a charity that helps people who do not have enough money to live. When he's not working, Mark spends time with his wife and four children. He also volunteers as a firefighter in New York state and works as a director at the Bezos Family Foundation. Mark's older brother, Jeff Bezos, is another of the directors.

1. Do you agree that Bezos probably cares about helping other people? Why?

2. What do you think Bezos's best memory of volunteering as a firefighter is? Why?

B Watch Mark Bezos's TED Talk once and check your answers to the questions in **A**. In pairs, discuss whether your ideas were right or wrong, and why.

C Watch the talk again. Circle the correct words in each sentence. Then, check your answers in pairs.

1. When he went to his *first / second* fire, Mark was the *first / second* volunteer.

2. The *man / woman* whose house was on fire did not have *an umbrella / any shoes*.

3. Another volunteer was told to go *inside / outside* and find the homeowner's *cat / dog*.

4. A few *weeks / months* after the fire, the homeowner sent the firefighters *an email / a letter*.

5. Mark suggests the audience could serve *drinks / food* or help clean up a *park / yard*.

D Complete the chart by listing some things that you could do to improve your life and / or somebody else's life.

Improve Your Life	
Improve Someone Else's Life	
Improve Your Life and Someone Else's Life	

E Ask your classmates what ideas they wrote. Make a note of the names of people who wrote at least one idea that is the same or similar to one of your ideas.

F Complete the steps.

1. Work with one of the people whose name you noted in exercise **E**.

2. Imagine you are really going to do one of the things on your list. Discuss and make notes about how you would do it, where and when you would do it, and why you would do it.

3. Put your notes in order to make a short talk. Then practice your talk, making sure you both speak.

4. Give your talk in front of the class. When it is your turn to listen to other students, take notes.

5. Join a different pair of students. Take turns using your notes to ask questions or give feedback to the other pair.

An endangered tree pangolin, with her
baby, at Pangolin Conservation in
St. Augustine, Florida

1 Why might these animals be endangered?

2 Are zoos and conservation centers the best way to save endangered species?

UNIT 5 GOALS

A. Say How Things Could Be Different

B. Discuss the Survival of Species

C. Talk about Threats to Survival

D. Discuss Rescues

E. Give Advice about Difficult Situations

GOAL Say How Things Could Be Different

Vocabulary

A Read the text. Then, discuss the meaning of the blue words with a partner.

One scientific study suggests that up to two billion different species may be alive now. That's a big number. However, since life began on Earth, scientists think at least *five* billion kinds of plants and animals have gone extinct. They know this from the discovery of many unknown kinds of fossils: dead plants or animals that have turned to stone.

Why did so many species not survive? Some species died out slowly because conditions changed. Others were killed in a huge natural disaster that happened about 66 million years ago. A big rock from space, called a comet, hit Earth. It killed the dinosaurs and caused terrible conditions. If humans had been alive at that time, they would have felt terror.

Many species are dying out these days, so some scientists think another mass extinction is happening now. They see a relationship between human activity and these deaths. For example, they think the problem is happening because humans are causing climate change. Is there any way to rescue species that are in danger? Maybe. If a scientist found a way to stop climate change, he or she would be a hero to people who care about the planet.

A young girl looks in amazement at a fossil dinosaur.

B In pairs, complete these definitions with a blue word from the text.

1. To _____ somebody is to save him or her from danger.

2. A _____ is a person who saves others or has a big effect on them.

3. _____ describes a plant or animal that died out, often a long time ago.

4. A _____ happens when somebody finds something that was lost.

5. A person who has experienced _____ has felt very strong fear.

6. A _____ is a link, or connection, between two people or events.

7. To _____ means to not die during a serious event.

8. A _____ is an event that creates terrible conditions and may cause many deaths.

9. _____ describes a plant or animal that is living, not dead.

10. _____ are groups of plants or animals that are similar in some ways.

C Expand your vocabulary by writing sentences using the noun forms of *extinct* and *survive*, the verb forms of *discovery* and *rescue*, and the adjective forms of *disaster* and *terror*. Work with a partner and use a dictionary if necessary.

Grammar

Unreal Conditionals

Use unreal conditionals to talk about a situation that is not true, but that could be (or could have been) true if something were different.	Dinosaurs are extinct, but if the comet had missed, they **might** be alive.
Unreal conditionals have two parts: a condition part and a result part. The order of the parts does not matter, but when the condition part is first, you need a comma.	If an earthquake happened, some buildings **might fall down**. Some buildings **might fall down** if an earthquake happened.
There are two kinds of unreal conditionals: • To discuss events that you think are unlikely (second conditonal). • To talk about events that are impossible (third conditional).	Many plants **would not grow** if bees died out. If dinosaurs had survived, they would have eaten all the humans.

D Underline the examples of unreal conditionals in the text in **A**. Then, rewrite the examples with the parts in the opposite order.

E In groups, fix the underlined mistakes in these unreal conditional sentences. Then discuss the sentences. How true do you think they are? Why?

1. We might learn more about the past if scientists <u>had discovered</u> more fossils.

2. If the big rock <u>missed</u> Earth 66 million years ago, dinosaurs might have survived.

3. Humans would be an endangered species if dinosaurs <u>are</u> still alive.

4. If climate change stopped getting worse, more species might <u>have lived</u>.

5. If a scientist stopped climate change, she <u>will</u> become rich and famous.

✔ GOAL CHECK Say How Things Could Be Different

Complete these sentences in your own words.

1. I would be happier if _____.

2. If I won a lot of money, I _____.

3. I could have _____ if I had _____.

4. If _____, I _____.

Then, interview your classmates and write the name of someone who wrote something that...

• is funny: _____.

• is unusual: _____.

• you wish you had written: _____.

• you hope comes true: _____.

> What did you write for the first sentence?

> I would be happier if I had more free time.

GOAL Discuss the Survival of Species

Listening

A Answer the questions in small groups.

1. What are fossils and how are they created? Share your knowledge.

2. When you were a child, how interested were you in fossils? Why?

3. You are going to listen to a talk about "living fossils." What do you think they are?

B 🎧 22 Listen to the first part of the talk and take notes. Then, in pairs, use your notes to confirm the answers to questions 1 and 3 in **A**.

C 🎧 23 Listen to the whole talk and complete the summaries with a number or word that the speaker says.

Horseshoe crabs are living fossils. They have been alive for (1) _____ of millions of years. They live off the (2) _____ Coast of the United States. They also live around China, (3) _____, Japan, Korea, and other parts of Southeast Asia. They look just like fossil horseshoe crabs.

Like horseshoe crabs, coelacanths are living fossils. They are a kind of (4) _____. Scientists believed they were extinct. Then, Marjorie Courtenay-Latimer discovered one in (5) _____. She was working for a (6) _____ in South Africa at the time.

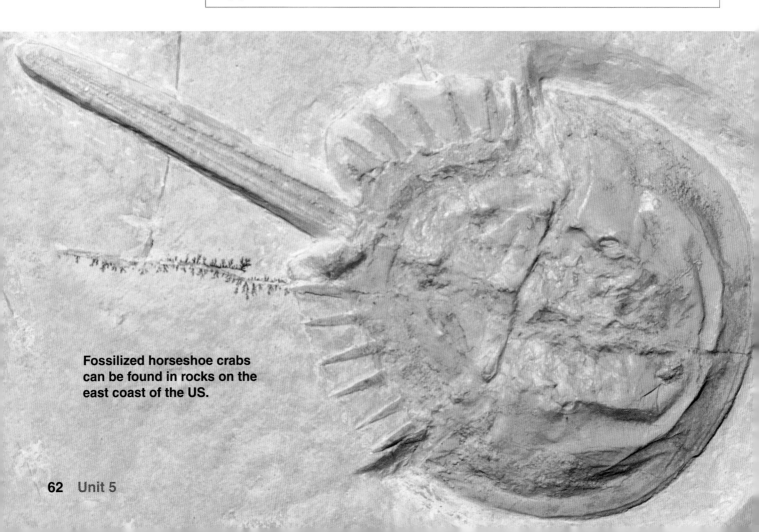

Fossilized horseshoe crabs can be found in rocks on the east coast of the US.

D Discuss these questions in a group.

1. How interesting did you find the talk about living fossils? Why?

2. Which of these living fossils would you most like to know more about: the volcano rabbit, vampire squid, or dinosaur ant? Why?

3. The speaker describes Marjorie Courtenay-Latimer as "a hero" because she was a woman doing science in the 1930s. Do you think "hero" is the right word in this case? Why?

PRONUNCIATION: Emphasis to Express Meaning

Speakers often emphasize a word to express a certain emotion or meaning. The exact emotion or meaning will depend on the emphasized word and on the situation.

- I **don't** like it. Please stop! (The emphasis probably shows anger.)
- You don't like it? **Really**? (The emphasis probably expresses surprise.)
- Actually, no, I **don't** like it. (The emphasis corrects a misunderstanding.)
- Jonah likes it, but **I** don't. (The emphasis makes the different opinions clear.)

E 🎧 24 Listen and underline the words that the speaker emphasizes. Then, in pairs, match each example of emphasis to one of the three reasons (a–c) below.

1. "Fossils are interesting, but today I want to focus on living fossils." _____

2. "In simple terms, these are species with three key... sorry, with two key characteristics." _____

3. "First, they're still alive now. And second, they look almost the same as actual fossils from long ago. They aren't the same, of course." _____

4. "Every species changes over time." _____

5. "However, living fossils look similar to their actual fossils because they have changed less than other species." _____

a. The emphasis corrects a mistake the speaker has made.

b. The emphasis contrasts one idea or thing with another one.

c. The emphasis makes sure listeners understand a key point.

✓ **GOAL CHECK** Discuss the Survival of Species

Complete these tasks. Use emphasis to express meaning during your discussions.

1. In groups, make a list of some important species that still exist. Discuss how your life might change if these species went extinct.

2. In different groups, make a list of species you know that have gone extinct. Discuss how the world would be different if these species were still alive.

C GOAL Talk about Threats to Survival

WILDFIRE

ERUPTION

HURRICANE

EARTHQUAKE

AVALANCHE

LANDSLIDE

FLOOD

DROUGHT

Has a natural disaster ever affected your country?

Language Expansion: Natural Disasters

A Look at the infographic. Then, complete these descriptions of natural disasters.

1. A _____ is a large storm that begins over the northern Atlantic Ocean.

2. A _____ is when little rain falls and there is not enough water.

3. A fire in the countryside that burns without stopping is a _____.

4. An explosion of rock, dust, and gas from a volcano is an _____.

5. When an _____ happens, the ground shakes and moves.

6. When mud, rock, and stones slide down a hill, it is called a _____.

7. When there is an _____, a lot of snow slides down a mountain.

8. When there is too much rain, a river or lake can cause a _____.

B Discuss this question in a small group.

WORD FOCUS

A **threat** is a dangerous thing that might happen.

Some people think natural disasters are becoming more common. Other people think the number of natural disasters is the same, but the media reports them more. Which way of thinking is more likely to be correct? Why?

C **MY WORLD** Write a list of things that you feel are a threat to your survival. Order the list from most to least dangerous. When you have finished, share your list with a partner. Which threats are on both of your lists?

Grammar

Using *wish* and *hope*	
Use *wish* (+ *that*) + subject + simple past verb to say that we want a present situation to be different. Using *wish* (+ *that*) + subject + past perfect suggests you are sorry about a specific situation.	I **wish (that)** earthquakes **didn't happen**. I **wish (that)** last year's earthquake **hadn't happened**.
Use *hope* (+ *that*) + subject + simple present verb to say that we want a situation to be different in the future, or to say what we want to happen.	I **hope (that)** we **get** no more earthquakes this year.

D In your notebook, complete these sentences in your own words. Then interview your classmates to find out their ideas. Which classmate's answers are most similar to yours?

> I hope that...   I wish that...   My family hopes...   My friends wish...

Conversation

E 🎧 25   In pairs, decide if you need *wish* or *hope* in each blank. Then, listen to check your answers.

Eric: Did you feel that earthquake last night? I thought I was going to get shaken out of bed! I (1)_____ that we don't get any more quakes. I hate them!

Tom: Me, too. Actually, I kind of (2)_____ we lived in a place that didn't have any natural disasters.

Mel: Well, I (3)_____ that you both knew more about safety.

Tom: What do you mean?

Mel: First of all, natural disasters can happen anywhere, so the danger is about the same wherever you live. And second, they're rare. You're much more likely to get hurt in a traffic accident.

Eric: Really? Well, I (4)_____ nothing bad happens to any of us—accident or natural disaster.

SPEAKING SRATEGY

Speakers often use **well** when they start speaking. We can use **well** to indicate:
- a thought about a question or statement.
- a change in topic.
- to rephrase something we have already said.

F Practice the conversation in groups of three. Then, talk about disasters you have heard about.

✓ GOAL CHECK Talk about Threats to Survival

In groups, complete the tasks and discuss the questions.

1. Share your lists of threats from **C**. How many natural disasters are on your lists?

2. In the conversation, Mel says traffic accidents are more dangerous than natural disasters. Based on this information, come up with a new list of everyday threats. Share your list with the class.

D GOAL Discuss Rescues

Reading

A Complete the tasks in small groups.

1. Share what you know about these events:
   - The rescue in 2018 of 12 boys and their coach after 17 days trapped in a cave in Thailand.
   - The rescue in 2010 of 33 men after 33 days trapped deep under the ground in Chile.
2. Discuss why you think these events became big news.

B Read the text. Complete each statement with one word from the text.

1. Night got trapped in a cave with friends from his soccer team on his _____.
2. Usually it is safe to enter the cave in _____, but the rains came early in 2018.
3. The boys' coach gave them his _____.
4. The team was discovered by three _____.
5. Over 100 _____ worked to get the boys out.

C Discuss these questions in groups.

1. The boys were all members of the same soccer team. Do you think this helped them survive?
2. This story became news around the world. Do you think this helped the team survive?
3. Do you think Saman Kunan was a hero? How about Coach Chantawong?

✓ GOAL CHECK

Work in a different group. If you were in these situations, what would you do? Explain and support your views.

- An earthquake traps 17 children in a building. Do you help dig them out?
- You see a whale on the beach. It's dying because it's too hot. Do you help keep the whale cool?
- You see a man in a fast-flowing river. He cannot swim. Do you try to help?
- A house is on fire. A person screams, "Save my dog!" Do you go into the house?

A Birthday to Remember

When he woke up on the morning of June 23rd, 2018, Peerapat Sompiangjai, whose nickname is "night," was excited. It was his seventeenth birthday, and his plans were to practice soccer and then have fun with friends from his team, the Wild Boars. When they fell asleep that night, however, Night and eleven of his friends felt hunger, thirst, and terror.

What happened? To celebrate Night's birthday, the Wild Boars explored the Tham Luang cave in northern Thailand. Their coach, Ekkapol Chantawong, went with them to keep them safe. Usually it is OK to explore the cave in June, but heavy summer rains suddenly started. The cave began filling with water and the Wild Boars had to go deeper into the cave to survive. They were **trapped**!

When the boys did not come home that evening, their parents became worried. They found the boys' bicycles, bags, and shoes outside the cave and **raised the alarm**. Soon, the story became big news around the world. **Volunteers** from many countries traveled to Thailand to help.

Inside the cave, the situation was not good. They had a little water, but almost no food. They did not know that people were looking for them. They did not even know what day it was or how long they had been trapped. Coach Chantawong tried to help the boys. He let them eat his share of the food, and he taught them how to **meditate** so they would feel less worried. He also told them to lie still in order to use less oxygen.

At last, there was good news on July 2nd, when three divers found the team alive. Around the world, people were happy to learn of their discovery. Now that divers

knew the boys' location, they could bring food, air, and medicine to them. However, the situation was not safe: the cave was full of water, the boys could not swim, and they were far from the cave entrance.

More heavy rains were expected, and the rescuers came up with a dangerous, desperate plan. First, they put diving equipment on the boys. Some divers then tied themselves to the boys and helped them swim to a dry part of the cave. Finally, more than 100 helpers took turns carrying the boys to the cave's entrance.

The plan was very dangerous, and sadly, diver Saman Kunan died while rescuing the boys. However, despite the danger, all of the Wild Boars, including Coach Chantawong, were out of the cave and being checked by doctors by July 10th. At last, after 17 days in the cave, they were all safe.

trapped in a situation or place with no way to get out
raise the alarm tell people about a dangerous situation
volunteers people who work or help without getting paid
meditate think and breathe in a calm, relaxing way

E

GOAL Give Advice about Difficult Situations

Communication

A Complete this information with prepositions from the box. Then, compare answers in pairs and discuss what natural disaster the advice is for.

after	during
for	from
inside	on
to	with

Before the Event

- Fix heavy furniture like bookcases or TVs (1) _____ walls or floors.
- Prepare an emergency box with enough food and water (2) _____ three days.

(3) _____ **the Event**

- If you are (4) _____ a building, stay where you are until the shaking stops.
- Cover your head and neck (5) _____ your arms or something protective.

(6) _____ **the Event**

- Move to a safe area that is far away (7) _____ things that could fall.
- If you are trapped, bang (8) _____ something till rescuers hear you.

People play golf while an ash plume is visible in the distance from the Kīlauea volcano on Hawaii's Big Island.

B In pairs, think of some social situations that are often difficult, such as starting a new job or giving somebody some bad news. Then, list the situations in order from the most to the least difficult.

COMMUNICATION SKILL: Giving Advice

When people are in a difficult situation, other people may give them advice. For advice about emergency situations, it is common to use imperative clauses.
   Cover your head.
   Move to a safe area.

Imperative clauses are very strong and direct, especially in spoken English. In non-emergency situations, it is more common to give advice using specific expressions or modals.
   It's a good idea to change computer passwords regularly.
   You might want to change your online passwords more often.

Writing

C Complete the steps in pairs.

an eruption   a fire   a flood   a hurricane

1. Your teacher will assign you one of the emergency situations in the box. Discuss what advice you could give for how to survive this emergency. Write your advice on a piece of paper.

2. Pass your paper to the pair of students on your left and take the paper from the students on your right. Read the advice and add any other ideas.

3. Repeat step 2 until your piece of paper has been returned to you.

4. Choose the three most useful pieces of advice on your paper. Share them with the class and explain why you chose them.

D In pairs, share your list of difficult situations from **B**. Discuss which kinds of situations are more difficult to survive: social situations like starting a new job, or physical dangers like natural disasters. Choose a situation—social or physical—that most of you have experienced.

E Write some advice for people who have to deal with the situation you chose. Then join a group and share your advice with other students. Discuss which advice you might follow if you were in that situation.

 GOAL CHECK Give Advice about Difficult Situations

Think of a difficult situation that you or somebody you know might have to deal with in the future. Take turns sharing your situation with the class and listening to the advice you get. Then say which advice was the most useful, and why.

THREE THINGS I LEARNED
WHILE MY PLANE CRASHED

RIC ELIAS
Entrepreneur,
CEO of Red Ventures

Ric Elias's **idea worth spreading** is that life can be changed in an instant, so don't delay. Be the best person you can be right now. Watch Elias's full TED Talk on TED.com.

A Look at the photo. Ric Elias was one of the people who survived when US Airways Flight 1549 landed on a river. In pairs, discuss what you know or can imagine about this flight.

B Number these events in the order you think they happened, from 1 to 6. Then watch the first part of the talk to check your answers.

_____ A flight attendant said the plane had hit some birds.

_____ The pilot turned the plane around to go back.

_____ The plane was silent after the engines were turned off.

_____ The plane's engines started to make a scary noise.

_____ The plane's pilot told everyone to "brace for impact."

_____ There was an explosion and smoke filled the plane.

US Airways Flight 1549 landed on the Hudson River, New York, US.

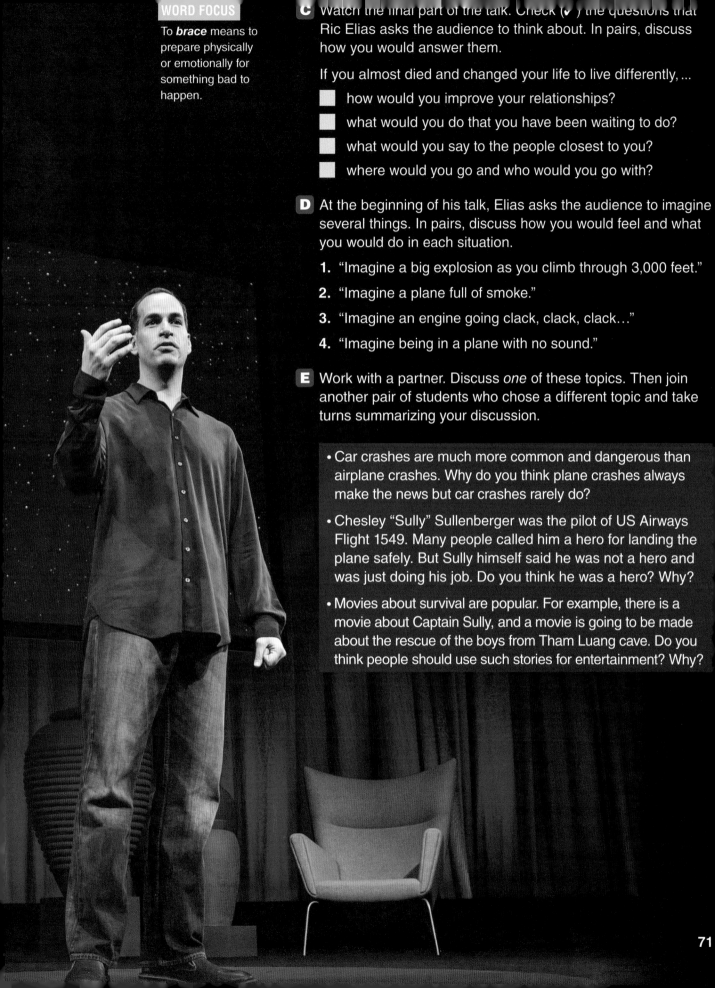

To **brace** means to prepare physically or emotionally for something bad to happen.

C Watch the final part of the talk. Check (✔) the questions that Ric Elias asks the audience to think about. In pairs, discuss how you would answer them.

If you almost died and changed your life to live differently, ...

▢ how would you improve your relationships?

▢ what would you do that you have been waiting to do?

▢ what would you say to the people closest to you?

▢ where would you go and who would you go with?

D At the beginning of his talk, Elias asks the audience to imagine several things. In pairs, discuss how you would feel and what you would do in each situation.

1. "Imagine a big explosion as you climb through 3,000 feet."

2. "Imagine a plane full of smoke."

3. "Imagine an engine going clack, clack, clack…"

4. "Imagine being in a plane with no sound."

E Work with a partner. Discuss *one* of these topics. Then join another pair of students who chose a different topic and take turns summarizing your discussion.

- Car crashes are much more common and dangerous than airplane crashes. Why do you think plane crashes always make the news but car crashes rarely do?

- Chesley "Sully" Sullenberger was the pilot of US Airways Flight 1549. Many people called him a hero for landing the plane safely. But Sully himself said he was not a hero and was just doing his job. Do you think he was a hero? Why?

- Movies about survival are popular. For example, there is a movie about Captain Sully, and a movie is going to be made about the rescue of the boys from Tham Luang cave. Do you think people should use such stories for entertainment? Why?

Alexa Meade's artwork
includes making
two-dimensional
representations of
people by painting
highlights and darks
on them.

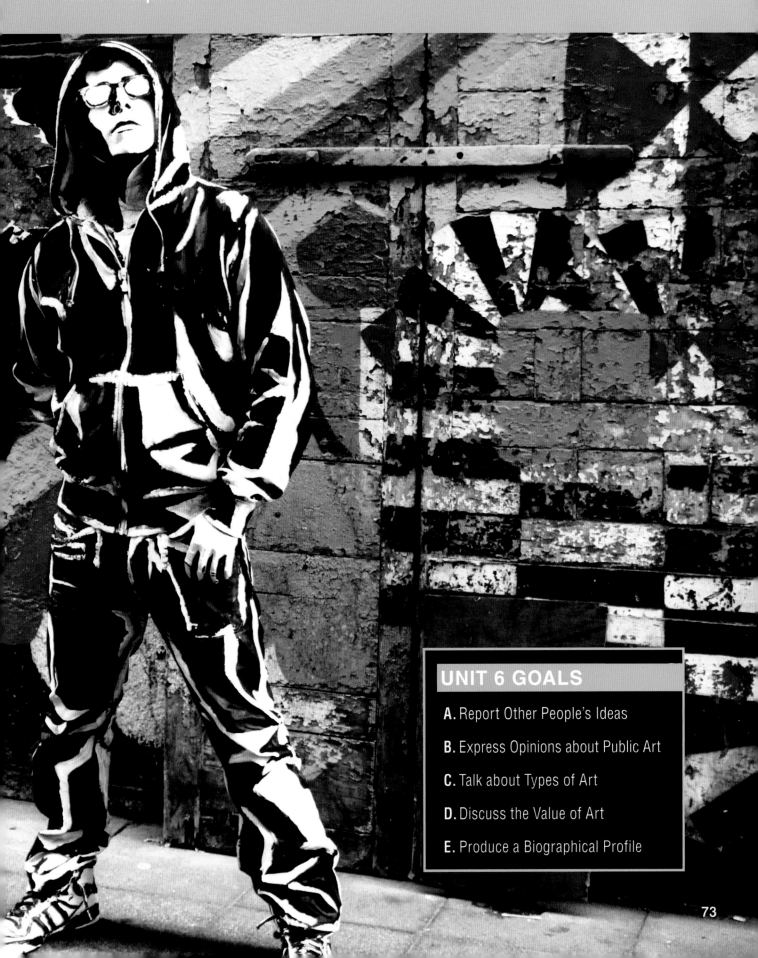

UNIT 6 GOALS

A. Report Other People's Ideas

B. Express Opinions about Public Art

C. Talk about Types of Art

D. Discuss the Value of Art

E. Produce a Biographical Profile

A GOAL Report Other People's Ideas

Vocabulary

A Read the text. In pairs, discuss what "great art" means to you.

Berthe Morisot (1841–1895), a French painter, was part of the Impressionist movement. This is one of her well-known pieces, called *A Woman Seated at a Bench on the Avenue du Bois.*

In general, artists are creative people who want their work to have an effect on those who see it. Great art can definitely inspire positive feelings. However, people's ideas about what "great art" is can change over time. For example, Impressionist art is now widely considered to be great. However, it was controversial for many years. People said that the style of painting and the use of color were too different from traditional art.

Modern art can be controversial, too. Take Andy Warhol's *Campbell's Soup Cans*. As the name suggests, it was 32 pictures of cans of soup. When it went on display at the Ferus Gallery in Los Angeles in 1962, some experts liked it, but many people said that it was not art. Carl Andre created another controversial piece of art: *Equivalent VIII* is an installation that is just a pile of bricks. The Tate, a famous gallery in London, England, bought the unique work in 1976. It was not expensive, but public reaction to the exhibition was negative. People expected to see portraits on the wall, not bricks on the floor. How will people feel about *Campbell's Soup Cans* and *Equivalent VIII* in the future? Will people think they are works of genius, or will their opinion be less positive? Only time will tell.

B In pairs, complete these definitions with a blue word from the text.

1. A _____ is a collection of art that people can look at.

2. A _____ is either a museum that displays art or a shop that sells art.

3. A _____ person is good at coming up with ideas or creating new things.

4. _____ is a special ability or a person who is very intelligent.

5. People have strongly contrasting views about something that is _____.

6. An _____ is art constructed inside a museum or in a public place.

7. Paintings or photographs of the face of a person are called _____.

8. Something that is _____ is different from other things because it is the only one of its kind.

9. To _____ is to give someone an idea that they want to do something.

10. An _____ is a special display of objects or artworks at a gallery or museum.

C Expand your vocabulary by finding the noun forms of *inspire*, *controversial*, and *creative*, and the verb forms of *installation*, *portrait*, and *display*.

Grammar

Reported Speech	
One way to report what somebody said is to quote his or her words. This is called *direct speech*.	**"I'm going to the gallery tomorrow,"** Sarah said. Paulo said, **"I'll go in a few weeks."**
Indirect speech is another way to report a person's words. In indirect speech, the original verb form usually changes—for example, from present to past—to make it clear that the person spoke at an earlier time. Some other original words, such as subject pronouns or time expressions, may also change.	Sarah said **(that) she was going to the gallery the next day**. Paulo said **(that) he would go a few weeks later**.

D Underline the examples of reported speech in the text in **A**.

E Rewrite these people's views in indirect speech.

1. Tom: "I think Leonardo da Vinci was a genius."

_____

2. Ann: "Banksy's art is controversial, but I like it."

_____

3. Bill: "The best kind of art is portraits of people."

_____

4. Zoe: "Galleries should be free so everyone can go."

_____

F In pairs, take turns reading the rewritten views in **E** aloud and saying how much you agree with each opinion.

 GOAL CHECK Report Other People's Ideas

In groups, complete the steps.

1. Interview your group members and note their answers to these questions.
- What do you think of Impressionist art like the work by Berthe Morisot?
- What do you think of Carl Andre's *Equivalent VIII*?
- What do you think of Andy Warhol's *Campbell's Soup Cans*?
- Should artists try to produce controversial art?

2. Find a partner from another group. Take turns sharing your interview answers using indirect speech.

GOAL Express Opinions about Public Art

Listening

A Read the text. Then, in small groups, discuss what you think of this art project and whether you would like a similar installation in your city.

> The city government today announced a new artwork for downtown. World-famous artist Zofira will turn the empty site where Truman's Department Store used to be into a giant ball pit that children and adults can enjoy. The installation is expected to be finished next spring. The project is being paid for by McKenzie and Company and Northern Trust Bank.

WORD FOCUS

To **argue for** something means to give and support an opinion about a topic.

B 🎧 27 Listen to a radio call-in show. Complete each opinion by writing the name of the person who expressed it: Ted, Linda, or Aziz.

1. _____ suggested the project could bring in money from tourists.

2. _____ argued that the project was a waste of the city's money.

3. _____ said that public art projects make cities more interesting.

4. _____ stated the city needed more public art projects, not fewer.

5. _____ explained that the project was bad for the environment.

6. _____ told the host that the project would make people happier.

People enjoy an interactive art installation made for adults in London, England.

C Which opinions from **B** are closest to your own? Why? Discuss in groups.

PRONUNCIATION: Thought Groups

When speaking, people usually divide their words into "thought groups" that express a single idea. In general:

- thought groups have a "focus word" that is given extra emphasis.
- speakers pause slightly at the end of each thought group, not in the middle.
- speakers often use falling intonation on the last word of each thought group.

She **said** // that the **art gallery** // was **amazing**.

D 🎧 **28** Say each sentence aloud, pausing at the // and paying attention to the focus words and intonation. Then listen and check your answers.

1. As far as I'm concerned, // it's a waste of money.

2. Real art is portraits // painted by geniuses // on display in galleries.

3. I think public art is important // because it adds character // to the city.

4. So, // from my perspective, // we need more public art, // not less.

E 🎧 **29** In pairs, discuss and mark the thought groups, focus words, and intonation in these sentences. Then, listen and check your answers.

Well, first, I'm sure the ball pit is going to bring a lot of tourists into the city. Those tourists will spend money, so the project will actually boost the economy. Also, I think the ball pit will make people in the city smile. And with so much bad news these days, we all need more fun, more laughter, don't you think?

✓ **GOAL CHECK** Express Opinions about Public Art

In groups, role-play the next part of the radio broadcast.

1. Decide who will play the role of the radio host and who will play the roles of people who call in to the show.

2. Decide what you will all say. The callers should express opinions about the ball pit installation. For example, a caller might argue that the city needs improvements to the public library instead of public art, or that the ball pit sounds fun. The host should introduce each caller and then react to what he or she says.

3. Write what you will say and practice.

4. Finally, perform your role play in front of the class. Which students expressed views you agree with? Which students expressed the most controversial views?

> Our next caller is Diego. Tell us what you think, please.

> Well, I don't like Zofira's work, so in my view...

Language Expansion: Types of Art

architecture
ceramic art
design
illustration
media art
painting
photography
sculpture

A Complete each definition with a word or phrase from the box. Then write the correct word or phrase next to the art type above.

1. _____ involves drawing an image of something on paper or a screen.

2. _____ involves making objects like pots or vases.

3. _____ is the act of using paint to make a picture.

4. _____ is the art of designing buildings and other structures.

5. _____ is the art of making objects from materials like stone or metal.

6. _____ is the art of taking beautiful or interesting photos with a camera.

7. _____ is the art of thinking of and making attractive and useful objects.

8. _____ uses different kinds of media, such as video and photographs.

B **MY WORLD** In small groups, discuss which of these types of art you have done in your life and which ones you most enjoy. Then discuss which ones you or your parents own, if any.

C In different small groups, choose two of these to add to the infographic and discuss how to define and illustrate them. Then share your ideas with the class.

| fashion | street art | literature | movies | music |

Grammar

Adjective Clauses 1

Adjective clauses, which are also called *relative clauses*, come after a noun and give additional information about it.	The architect **who / that created the building** just won an award.
Sometimes an adjective clause gives extra information that is necessary in order to understand which person or thing the sentence refers to. These clauses are written *without* commas.	The artist **who / that sculpted this** is from Mexico. I love the illustration **that / which is on page 27**.
Sometimes an adjective clause gives extra information that is unnecessary because it is clear which person or thing the sentence refers to (even without the clause). These clauses are written *with* commas.	This gallery, **which opened last year**, has a great display of ceramic art. My sister, **who is two years older than me**, is a furniture designer.

D Complete these sentences by writing *who*, *which*, or *that* in the correct spaces. Then, compare answers in pairs.

- Use (1) _____ (or (2) _____) to introduce an adjective clause that gives more information about a person.
- Use (3) _____ (or (4) _____) to introduce an adjective clause which gives more information about a thing.
- Use only (5) _____ or (6) _____ in adjective clauses that give additional, unnecessary information, not (7) _____.

Conversation

E 🎧 30 In pairs, decide if you need *who*, *which*, or *that* in each blank. Then listen to check your answers.

Ella: My friend Ben, _____ works at the art gallery, told me about some new controversial art. Do you want to go see it?

Hiro: Controversial art? Like what?

Ella: Well, there's a work called *Equivalent VIII*, _____ is just a pile of bricks on the floor, by American artist Carl Andre. And Ben said that *Cambell's Soup Cans*, _____ I really want to see, is on display, too.

Hiro: What? Soup cans? Why are soup cans in a gallery?

Ella: No, I mean *Campbell's Soup Cans* by the artist Andy Warhol, _____ is American.

Hiro: Really? Cans don't sound much like art to me, but I'd like to see the exhibition!

SPEAKING STRATEGY

Use adjective clauses to give additional information about a topic.

✓ GOAL CHECK Talk about Types of Art

Look at the types of art in **A** and **C** and pick your three favorite and least favorite. Then, share your opinions in groups, giving reasons for your views.

GOAL Discuss the Value of Art

Reading

A **MY WORLD** In small groups, say whether you have ever bought or sold anything using an online auction site. Explain your reasons.

B In groups, read the title of the text and discuss what you think it means. Then scan the text to find which paragraph explains the meaning.

C Read the text. Which paragraph has each piece of information?

_____ **1.** A controversy about who painted *Salvator Mundi*

_____ **2.** An explanation of the two kinds of value art has

_____ **3.** How much Griffin spent on two paintings

_____ **4.** The location of the Isabella Stewart Gardner Museum

_____ **5.** The period during which Maezawa spent $98 million

_____ **6.** The record price for art in 1987

_____ **7.** An explanation of what makes artworks rare

_____ **8.** Why it is bad if galleries cannot afford art

D In small groups, look at the picture and describe what you see. Then discuss what you know about Van Gogh.

 GOAL CHECK

Complete the tasks in groups.

1. The text discusses two different meanings for "the value of art." What are they? Can you think of any other values that art has?

2. What is the value of art for these people?
- You and your friends
- Very rich people
- Young children
- Artists

The Art Bubble

Vincent van Gogh painted his famous work of art, *Irises*, in 1889.

A At an art auction in 1987, *Irises* by Vincent van Gogh was sold. The price made headlines around the world because it was a record for a piece of art. Some people said that $53.9 million was too much. They claimed that art prices would stop going up. They argued that the art bubble would pop. They were wrong.

B Over the years, art prices continued to go up and up and up again. Then, 30 years later, in 2017, *Salvator Mundi* by Leonardo da Vinci was auctioned. The buyer paid $450.3 million. This price broke the previous record by more than $150 million. It also raises some questions: Is any painting worth so much money? Who can pay so much for art, and why do they do it? And what is next for the art world? In other words, will prices continue to rise, or will the art bubble pop and prices fall?

C In the past, galleries usually bought important works to put on display for the public. These days, however, only the super-rich can afford to buy major pieces. For example, Kenneth C. Griffin, who is a wealthy American, spent more than half a billion dollars to buy just two paintings. And Yusaku Maezawa, a Japanese billionaire, spent $98 million on art in just two days in 2016.

D Why do these people pay so much? First, many artworks are unique. This makes them rare, and throughout history people have always paid more for rare things than common ones. Second, works of art are beautiful, and humans have always been willing to pay for beauty.

E Are these paintings worth their sky-high prices? From an emotional point of view, the answer may be *yes* if the buyer truly loves the work. And from a financial point of view, the answer may also be *yes*; art prices continue to rise, so buying art may seem like a good **investment**. This may not be true in every case, however. For example, the idea that Leonardo da Vinci painted *Salvator Mundi* is controversial. Some experts say that it was most likely painted by one of his students. If this is true, the work's value could drop hugely.

F Many experts think that the art bubble will not pop any time soon, which is bad news for society. Art has both a financial value and a cultural value, and if people cannot see great works of art, they will see less beauty and fewer examples of creative genius. Perhaps fewer people will become artists because the art in galleries does not inspire them. We must hope that those who pay $100 million or more for art will follow the example of Jack Gardner and his wife Isabella Stewart Gardner. They were wealthy collectors who opened a museum in Boston to put their art on display for the public.

investment something that can bring money in the future

Communication

A In groups, make a list of the five most famous artists you know. Then discuss these questions.

1. How many of your listed artists are men? Does this number surprise you? Why?

2. How many of the artists are still alive? Does this number surprise you? Why?

3. Where do the artists come from? Are people from some countries better at art than people from other countries? Why do you think so?

B In different groups, say which of these three works of art you like most, and why. Then, read the three profiles and discuss which artist probably painted each work.

A

B

C

1. **Élisabeth Vigée Le Brun** was born in France in 1755 and died in 1842. She had so much talent that she made money from painting when she was still a teenager. In fact, although many great portrait artists lived during this period, she was very successful. Vigée Le Brun is most famous for her portraits of famous women, such as Marie Antoinette, the Queen of France.

2. **Ōi Katsushika** was born around 1800 and died about 66 years later. Her father was Hokusai, one of the most famous of all Japanese artists. However, like him, she was a gifted artist who painted works in a style called *ukiyo-e*. She was famously good at painting women, but also painted scenes of nature and daily life in Japan.

3. **Mary Cassatt** was born in the US in 1844. She wanted to become an artist, so she moved to France when she was 22. She lived most of the rest of her life there until her death in 1926. While there, Cassatt met and was influenced by impressionist artists like Edgar Degas and Claude Monet. She began to paint portraits and natural scenes in the impressionist style.

C Look at the profiles of the three artists again. In pairs, check (✓) the information that some or all of the profiles include. Underline examples.

☐ A comparison of the artist and one or more other artists

☐ A description of at least one important work by the artist

☐ A description of the artist's painting style and usual topics

☐ A discussion of the cost and value of the artist's major works

☐ A discussion of the people or ideas that influenced the artist

☐ An explanation of where and when the artist was born

Writing

D Read the information about referring to research. Then complete the steps.

COMMUNICATION SKILL: Referring to Research

Before writing something or giving a talk, you may need to research your topic first.

- When you research, make sure you use sources (e.g., books or websites) that you can trust. Also, try to find at least two sources to support each point you want to make or fact you want to include; if you have just one source, the information may be inaccurate.

- When you refer to your research when writing or speaking, use either direct or indirect speech to report people's words or opinions. You should also say where you found the information.

---

1. Choose an artist whose work you like. Research information about his or her life.

2. Using your research notes, write a first draft of a short biographical profile of the artist. Use the profiles in **B** as a guide.

3. Share your profile with a partner and give each other feedback about how to improve it.

4. Use your partner's feedback to write a better second draft. Then submit it.

 GOAL CHECK Produce a Biographical Profile

Choose one of these situations and write a short biographical profile of yourself. Include the appropriate details for the situation you have chosen. When you have finished, share your profile with a group. Can your partners guess which situation you chose?

- A profile to enter an art competition
- A profile for a job application
- A profile for a social media account
- A profile for a television show audition

VIDEO JOURNAL

ANTARCTICA: WHILE YOU WERE SLEEPING

A In groups, look at the photo and read the quotation from Joseph Michael, an artist from New Zealand. Answer the questions.

1. What type of artist do you think Joseph Michael is? Would you like to be this kind of artist? Why?

2. What does the quotation mean? How true do you think it is? Why?

B Watch the video without sound and take notes. Then complete the tasks.

1. In pairs, discuss what the video shows. Work together to write a short description.

2. Share your description with the class and listen to other students' descriptions. Discuss the best parts from all the descriptions.

C Watch the video again, with sound. Take notes. Then, work in small groups. How accurate was your description from **B**?

D In pairs, correct the mistakes in these statements.

1. Michael describes himself as a media artist who hates adventure.

2. Michael and his team spent two months around the Antarctic Peninsula.

3. The art project took two years.

4. Michael tested his art on models of the iceberg.

5. Michael says that the process of creating his art was like peeling an apple.

E Rank these these opinions from the video in order of how much you agree with them (from most to least). In groups, share and explain the order you chose.

a. Photography [is] the most simple, simplistic form of art.

b. Art is about doing complex things for a simple reason.

c. Especially with ... art, it's really important that people feel something.

d. The biggest thing about being an artist ... is you got to have that lack of fear of failure.

F Discuss these questions in groups.

1. Do you think Michael's art would have a big impact on people if it were shown indoors?

2. Some people might say that Michael's art is a waste of time and money. Do you agree?

3. Which piece of art from this unit do you like the most? Why?

WORD FOCUS

A **lack of** means something is not available or there is not enough of it.

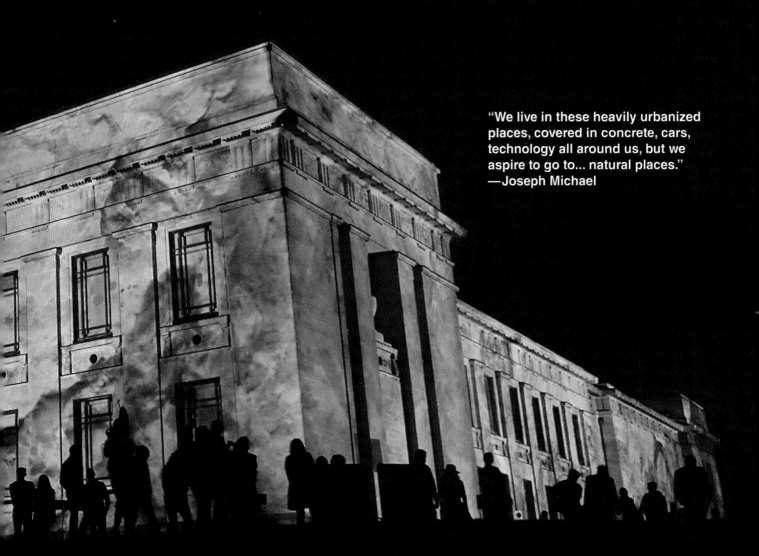

"We live in these heavily urbanized places, covered in concrete, cars, technology all around us, but we aspire to go to... natural places."
—Joseph Michael

Getting Around

The Seattle Center Monorail in the state of
Washington, US passes through the Museum
of Pop Culture designed by Frank O. Gehry.

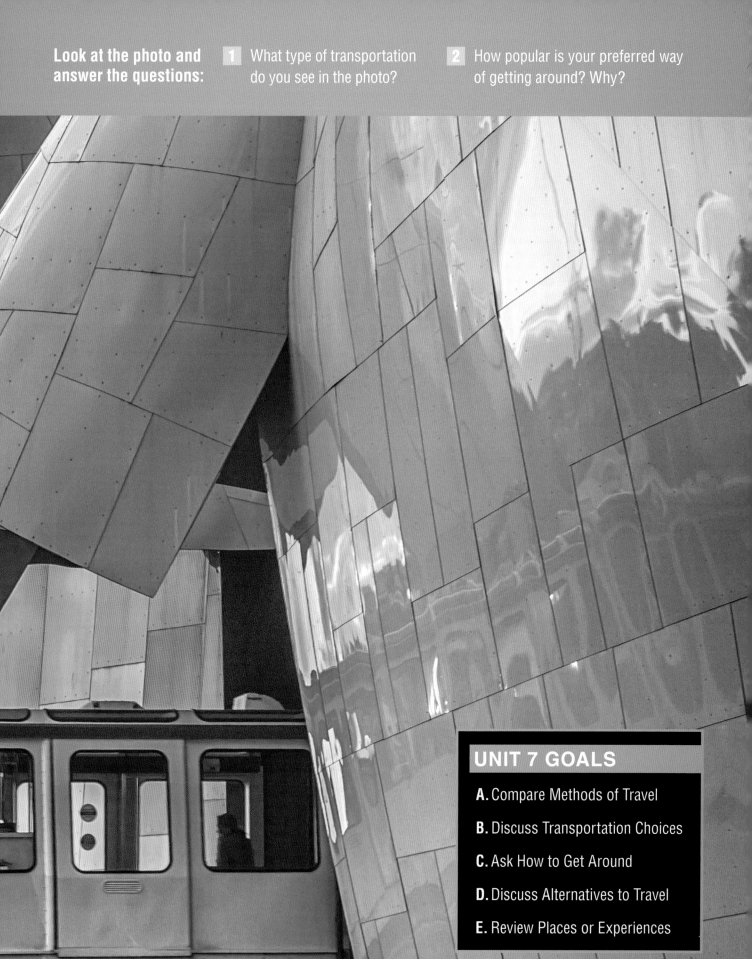

Look at the photo and answer the questions:

1 What type of transportation do you see in the photo?

2 How popular is your preferred way of getting around? Why?

UNIT 7 GOALS

A. Compare Methods of Travel

B. Discuss Transportation Choices

C. Ask How to Get Around

D. Discuss Alternatives to Travel

E. Review Places or Experiences

87

GOAL Compare Methods of Travel

Vocabulary

The History of Getting Around

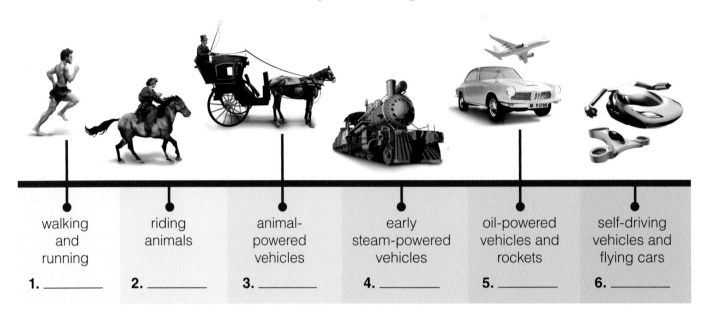

walking and running	riding animals	animal-powered vehicles	early steam-powered vehicles	oil-powered vehicles and rockets	self-driving vehicles and flying cars
1. _____	2. _____	3. _____	4. _____	5. _____	6. _____

A In pairs, discuss which paragraph (a–f) describes each part of the graphic (1–6).

a. A few hundred years ago, the first steam vehicles were built. Steam allowed people to travel farther and faster than ever before. Then oil was discovered as a useful fuel. This led to the development of cars and other motor vehicles.

b. After all these developments, what will human transportation be like in the future? Will self-driving vehicles and flying cars become common? Will humans explore Mars or other planets? Time will tell.

c. After the wheel was developed, carts and other kinds of simple vehicles could be built. These could be used for travel by several passengers at the same time.

d. In the early twentieth century, the first aircraft were built. Cars, buses, and trains became faster, too. This allowed people to live in one place and commute to a job in a different place. In the middle of the twentieth century, scientists developed rockets to launch satellites into space.

e. Later, people learned to ride animals such as horses or camels. Riding made it easier to reach a distant destination, but many journeys still took a long time.

f. The earliest humans could only get around by walking or running. As a result, places that were a long distance away could not be reached easily.

Do you know what *commute* means?

Yes, it means to travel regularly from your home to work and back.

B 🎧 32 Complete each definition with one of the words in blue in **A**. Then, listen to check your answers.

1. _____ a system for moving people from one place to another

2. _____ a material people burn or use to make energy

3. _____ a machine that can fly, such as an airplane or helicopter

4. _____ go from home to work or school, and then back again

5. _____ go to and travel around a place to learn more about it

6. _____ put something into space or the sky; start something new

7. _____ people who take trips in or on vehicles

8. _____ trips, especially long ones, from one place to another

9. _____ the amount of space between two places or two things

10. _____ the place somebody is going or something is being sent

C Expand your vocabulary by learning the noun form of *commute* (two forms) and *launch*, the verb form of *fuel*, *journey*, and *transportation*, and the adjective form of *distance*.

Grammar

The Passive 3	
Use modals in passive (or active) sentences to indicate: 1. necessity (*must*) 2. possibility (*might*, *may*, or *could*) 3. ability (*could* [past ability] or *can*) Notice the placement of the modal in the passive constructions.	1. Your passport **must** be shown. (passive) You **must** show your passport. (active) 2. The flight **might** be delayed. (passive) They **might** delay the flight. (active) 3. Tickets **can** be bought here. (passive) You **can** buy tickets here. (active)

D Read the grammar information. Then, in pairs, underline each example of a passive construction with a modal in **A**. Circle each example of a passive without a modal.

 GOAL CHECK Compare Methods of Travel

In groups, complete the steps.

1. Choose one of the methods of transportation shown in the graphic in **A**. Discuss its good points, its bad points, and how it compares with other methods of travel.

2. Prepare and practice a short talk that compares the method of travel you chose with two other ways to travel. Include some passive constructions with modals in your talk.

3. Deliver your talk to the class. Make sure each member of your group speaks.

GOAL Discuss Transportation Choices

A Read the information. In pairs, discuss which benefits of self-driving cars you have heard before. Also say which two benefits are most important to you and why.

Many experts think self-driving vehicles (SDVs) will soon be a common sight on our roads. They feel this is likely because SDVs have many benefits over normal vehicles:

air quality – SDVs drive more efficiently, so they create less pollution.

open cities – SDVs can park in small spaces, so parking lots could become real parks.

personal time – SDV passengers do not drive, so they can spend travel time as they like.

safety – Machines make fewer errors than people, so more SDVs will mean fewer accidents.

travel cost – Private vehicles cost a lot; SDVs may allow people to share the cost of a vehicle.

Listening

B 🎧 33 Listen to the first part of an interview with an expert in self-driving vehicles. Circle **T** for *true* or **F** for *false*. In pairs, correct the false statements.

1. The company's self-driving car crossed the country from east to west only.	**T**	**F**
2. The human sitting in the self-driving car did not have to operate it even once.	**T**	**F**
3. The man develops self-driving vehicles, but he is not especially interested in cars.	**T**	**F**
4. The man became interested in self-driving cars after a talk by one of his friends.	**T**	**F**
5. The talk was about developing artificial intelligence to let cars drive themselves.	**T**	**F**

WORD FOCUS

Artificial intelligence refers to computer systems capable of performing tasks usually undertaken by humans.

A man in an autonomous driving test vehicle

Autonomous Mode

C 🎧 34 Listen to the rest of the interview. Which of the benefits of self-driving vehicles from **A** does the expert mention?

D In groups, discuss what each quotation from the interview means. Also, discuss how true you think each quotation is and why.

1. "[The development area of SDV] sounded like an exciting field."
2. "Safety will come when we have *more* self-driving cars on the road."
3. "[Self-driving vehicles will be common] in the next ten years."
4. "These vehicles are great as people can work while they travel."

PRONUNCIATION: Reduced Auxiliaries *Are* and *Have*

In spoken English, auxiliary verbs like *are* and *have* are usually reduced. In the middle of a sentence, *are* often sounds like /ər/ (*uh*), and *have* can sound like /əv/ (*of*).

> She thinks buses **are** slow. ➔ she thinks buses **uh** slow
>
> We should **have** taken the train. ➔ we should **of** taken the train

---

E 🎧 35 Listen to these sentences from the interview. <u>Underline</u> the auxiliaries that are reduced. Then, practice saying the sentences naturally.

1. "You have a car that drives itself across the country, and you could have focused on that."
2. "The thing is, cars driven by humans are *more* dangerous than self-driving cars are."
3. "I'm sure many other people have felt the same way about traffic jams."
4. "So, these vehicles are great because people can work while they travel."

F In groups, make a list of different vehicles, such as cars, buses, and planes. Then discuss some benefits and problems of using each vehicle. Use reduced auxiliaries when it is natural to do so.

✓ **GOAL CHECK** Discuss Transportation Choices

Complete the steps.

1. Interview several classmates. Ask them which vehicles they have used recently and why they chose each one.

2. Interview several different classmates. Ask them which vehicles they plan to use in the future and why.

3. In groups, compare your interview results and discuss these questions:
   • Which vehicles have people used most often recently?
   • Which vehicles are people most likely to use in the future?
   • What reasons for choosing a type of vehicle were most common?
   • Does the number of people who plan to use self-driving vehicles surprise you?

GOAL Ask How to Get Around

Language Expansion: Public Transportation

A In pairs, discuss the meaning of the words in the box. Use a dictionary if necessary. Then complete the text with them. One word is extra.

board	fares	transit
passes	routes	terminals
tickets	transfer	travel

The Bus Rapid (1) _____ (BRT) system of Curitiba, Brazil, is famous for its convenience and design. The buses are big enough for up to 250 passengers, and they travel all around the city. People wait for buses in cool-looking, tube-shaped stations. And if they don't have (2) _____, they pay their (3) _____ in the station. This saves time because everyone can (4) _____ the bus quickly when it arrives. The system lets passengers (5) _____ to other lines without paying again. Where different (6) _____ connect, there are comfortable (7) _____ with small shops and restrooms. The system is fast and efficient. It is also relatively inexpensive, especially for passengers who buy weekly or yearly (8) _____. As a result, the BRT is not only popular among people who live in Curitiba, but also with those who visit the city.

B **MY WORLD** In groups, discuss the questions. In general, do you enjoy using public transportation? Why? How does the BRT system compare with public transportation in a city you know well?

Conversation

C 🎧 36 Read the grammar information on the following page. Then complete the conversation by writing *how*, *where*, or *whether* in each space. Then listen to check your answers.

SPEAKING STRATEGY

Use indirect questions to be polite. Sometimes these phrases start the question:

Excuse me, ...

Sorry to ...

Edson: Excuse me, do you know (1)_____ the next bus goes to the airport?

Tracy: It depends. The number 27 bus goes to the airport, but the 28 doesn't.

Edson: I see. And (2) _____ much is the fare?

Tracy: A one-way ticket costs $3. A return ticket is one dollar more.

Edson: Sorry to keep bothering you, but I'd also like to know (3) _____ long it takes.

Tracy: To get to the airport? It depends on the traffic, but usually it's about 20 minutes.

Edson: That's great. Thanks for your help.

Tracy: No problem ... You must be a visitor. (4) _____ are you from?

Edson: I'm from Curitiba in Brazil. Do you know it?

Tracy: I've heard of it ... Oh, look. A bus is coming. Can you tell (5) _____ it's the 27 or the 28?

Grammar

Indirect Questions

Indirect questions are questions inside other questions or statements. The last content word usually has falling intonation.	Could you tell me where the station is? I was wondering why you took a taxi.
Because people think indirect questions are polite, they often use them when talking to a person they do not know well.	When does the bus leave? (direct) Do you know when the bus leaves? (indirect)
Use statement word order in indirect questions, not question word order.	I'd like to know where the subway station is. ~~I'd like to know where is the subway station.~~
Use *if* or *whether* in indirect *yes / no* questions.	Do you know if / whether the flight is on time?

D Complete the tasks in pairs.

1. Underline indirect questions in the conversation in **C**. Rewrite direct questions as indirect ones.

2. Take turns practicing the roles in the conversation.

3. Extend the conversation by adding two more comments by each speaker. Include at least one indirect question. Then practice the new conversation.

 GOAL CHECK Ask How to Get Around

Think about how you would answer these questions:
- Where is your favorite restaurant?
- What is a relaxing place you like to visit?

- Where is one place you love shopping?
- What is one fun, free place that you know?

Interview another student. If you know the person, ask direct questions; if not, use indirect questions. If you do not know the place, ask direct or indirect questions to find out how to get there.

BRT bus stop in
Curitiba, Brazil

D GOAL Discuss Alternatives to Travel

Reading

A In small groups, look at the photo and discuss how you feel about virtual reality (VR) headsets.

B Read the text. Circle the reason why the author wrote each sentence.

1. "We commute to work, visit friends, or go shopping."

   a. To give some typical examples of daily travel

   b. To describe a typical person's daily routine

2. "And vacations can also be surprisingly stressful."

   a. To contrast two opinions about a topic

   b. To add a further example of a problem

3. "These are vacations in which you stay at home."

   a. To suggest an action people often enjoy

   b. To define a term people may not know

4. "Still, for many people, reading or watching a show about a place is a poor alternative to going there."

   a. To introduce a problem about one topic

   b. To compare ways to deal with an issue

5. "A "traveler" puts on a VR headset and runs special software."

   a. To describe part of a process

   b. To emphasize a major difficulty

6. "Still, one major hotel chain already gives its guests the chance to enjoy VR travel in their rooms."

   a. To suggest something is already popular

   b. To contrast a previous negative point

GOAL CHECK

In small groups, discuss what you think a *nearcation* is. Then think of reasons to persuade someone who really needs a vacation to take one of these alternatives to a traditional vacation. Present your reasons to the class. Which group's reasons were the best?

- a staycation
- a nearcation
- an armchair traveler
- a VR (travel) experience

The Future of "Travel"?

Most of us travel each day. We commute to work, visit friends, or go shopping. This kind of travel may be necessary, but it is not always fun. As a result, most of us also look forward to traveling somewhere for a relaxing vacation. In theory, traveling is a wonderful experience. In practice, however, there can be problems with taking a trip.

Cost is one issue. Vacations can be expensive, especially for people with children. Another problem is time. In the modern world, many of us are too busy to take a relaxing trip away. And vacations can also be surprisingly stressful. We might have to deal with lost luggage, unfamiliar food, large crowds, noisy hotel rooms, or uncomfortable aircraft seats. And to top it all off, long-distance flights are bad for the environment because aircraft burn a lot of fuel.

Because of these problems, staycations have become more popular. These are vacations in which you stay at home. During a staycation, people will often visit nearby tourist attractions. They may also do other fun things such as eat at restaurants more than usual, visit shopping malls, or go to local festivals. And because people do not have to fly to a distant destination or stay in a hotel, staycations cost less than vacations.

However, staycations are not a perfect solution. For one thing, visiting tourist sites and eating out is not cheap. Some people overcome this problem by choosing to

be "armchair travelers." They take a staycation, but instead of spending money to visit nearby attractions or restaurants, they read books or watch documentaries about other places. The cost is very low, of course. Still, for many people, reading or watching a show about a place is a poor alternative to going there.

Virtual reality may offer a high-tech way for us to "see" the world. A "traveler" puts on a VR headset and runs special software. The software takes her on a "journey" to another place, such as the mountains of Chile. The VR traveler feels she is really in that place. By turning her head, for instance, she will see mountains behind or in front. The software may also let her "interact" with things. For example, she may be able to "pick up" something to look at it more closely.

VR travel is not a perfect solution, either. The VR experience may be enjoyable and realistic in some ways, but it is not the same as being there. And psychology studies show that having real experiences is important for our happiness. Still, one major hotel chain already gives its guests the chance to enjoy VR travel in their rooms. And the technology will get better. Perhaps in the near future, VR will give us the chance to "explore" the moon or Mars.

Communication

A Read the three reviews and choose the best title and star rating from the box. Then, in pairs, compare answers. One answer is extra.

> A little-known treasure! Wow! ★★★★   Some good things, some bad ★★☆☆
>
> Great... in the right season ★★★☆   Don't trust the other reviews ★☆☆☆

There are a lot of great things to say about the resort. The staff was friendly and helpful, the rooms were clean and comfortable, and the facilities were top quality. Why not four stars? We came at the wrong time of year. In winter, I'm sure there's a lot to do. In summer, though, a lot of shops and tourist attractions are closed, which is too bad.

We chose this hotel based on a lot of really positive four-star reviews. I think people must have been paid to write those reviews because the reality was very different. The rooms were dirty, the food was bad, the pools were closed, and the service was terrible. I can honestly say it was my worst vacation ever, and I wish I had stayed home. I'm going to try to get my money back.

I discovered this hotel online but couldn't find any reviews, so I took a chance... and I'm glad I did. It was fantastic. It's smaller than the other hotels on the beach, but the staff really try to make sure each guest is happy. The rooms aren't large, but they're quiet and beautiful. And the views from the windows are just incredible. It was so amazing that I'm going back next year, too!

Sunset on the coast of the Spanish island Tenerife.

B Discuss the questions in groups.

1. The reviews in **A** are for hotels. What other things do people often review?

2. In your view, how much do people rely on reviews when they travel to other places?

3. Writing reviews takes time. What are some reasons people decide to write them?

4. One reviewer said, "People must have been paid to write those reviews." Why are paid reviews a problem?

C **MY WORLD** In pairs, take turns talking about a time when you either wrote a review because of a good or bad experience, or trusted a review when making a decision.

Writing

COMMUNICATION SKILL: Expressing and Supporting Opinions

In both writing and speaking, it is common to give an opinion about a topic and support it with details and examples. You can express and support your opinion in several ways:

* directly by using specific expressions such as *In my view* or *For me.*
* directly by using positive or negative adjectives such as *great* or *terrible.*
* semi-directly by contrasting one thing with something better or worse.
* indirectly by mentioning your plans, hopes, or wishes about the topic.

D In groups, read the reviews in **A** again. Then, underline examples of each method of expressing and supporting an opinion described in the box.

 GOAL CHECK Review Places or Experiences

Complete the tasks.

1. Write *one* of these three reviews: (1) a transportation company you have used, such as an airline or railway; (2) a place you have visited, such as a country, city, or hotel; or (3) an experience you have had, such as a music concert or meal at a restaurant.

2. Write your name on your review but do not include a star rating. Put your review in a place where other students can read it.

3. Read several reviews by other students. Make a note of who wrote each review. Also note the star rating you think the review should have, from one star (terrible) to four (amazing).

4. Talk to the students who wrote the reviews you read. Say what star rating you think the review should have, and why. Then listen to the star rating each writer would give.

TEDTALKS

SpaceX'S PLAN TO FLY YOU ACROSS THE GLOBE IN 60 MINUTES

A You are going to watch an interview between Chris Anderson, from TED, and Gwynne Shotwell, a rocket engineer. Discuss these questions in groups.

1. Read the **idea worth spreading**. What do you think it means?

2. Look at the large photo. What do you think it shows?

B Early in the TED Talk, Anderson asks Shotwell how she became an engineer. In pairs, predict what influenced her. Then, watch the first part of the interview to check your answers.

a. ☐ attending an engineering event

b. ☐ having a childhood interest in cars

c. ☐ reading a book she was given

d. ☐ her teacher from the third grade

e. ☐ clothes another engineer wore

f. ☐ the work one of her parents did

C Watch the second part of the talk and circle the correct answers.

1. The Big Falcon Rocket can put satellites *8 / 18 / 80* meters in diameter into orbit.

2. Journeys between cities on the Big Falcon Rocket may take up to *20 / 90 / 40* minutes.

3. The first Big Falcon Rocket will have space for around *10 / 100 / 1,000* passengers.

4. Unlike aircraft, the Big Falcon Rocket can travel *a few / several / dozens of* times a day.

5. The Big Falcon Rocket may fly between major cities within the next *2 / 10 / 20* years.

GWYNNE SHOTWELL
Engineer, President, and COO of SpaceX

Gwynne Shotwell's **Idea Worth Spreading** is that rockets could improve travel on Earth as well as making it possible for humans to travel to other planets.

D Watch the final part of the interview. Circle **T** for *true* or **F** for *false*. Then, in pairs, compare answers and correct false statements.

1. SpaceX plans to use the Big Falcon Spaceship to fly humans to Mars.   **T**   **F**

2. On average, the trip to Mars currently takes two to three months.   **T**   **F**

3. Gwynne Shotwell says the first human will land on Mars next year.   **T**   **F**

4. Some people believe that SpaceX should fix Earth, not travel to Mars.   **T**   **F**

5. Shotwell gives one reason why she thinks humans should go to Mars.   **T**   **F**

E In small groups, complete the tasks.

1. Discuss your reactions to each of the three parts of the interview between Chris Anderson and Gwynne Shotwell.

2. Shotwell explains what influenced her to become an engineer. Share some of the people and things that have influenced your life so far.

3. Shotwell says that the Big Falcon Rocket could take people from one city to another in less than an hour. Discuss the advantages and disadvantages of this new way of getting around.

4. SpaceX is planning to carry humans to Mars. Discuss whether you would like to travel to Mars in the future.

F Work in a different group. Many people have a negative opinion about long-distance travel. Come up with three things that SpaceX could do to make passengers on the Big Falcon Rocket and the Big Falcon Spaceship comfortable. Then share your ideas with the class.

WORD FOCUS

To **influence** people means to change how they think or act.

Soccer fans react to
a World Cup game
in Berlin, Germany.

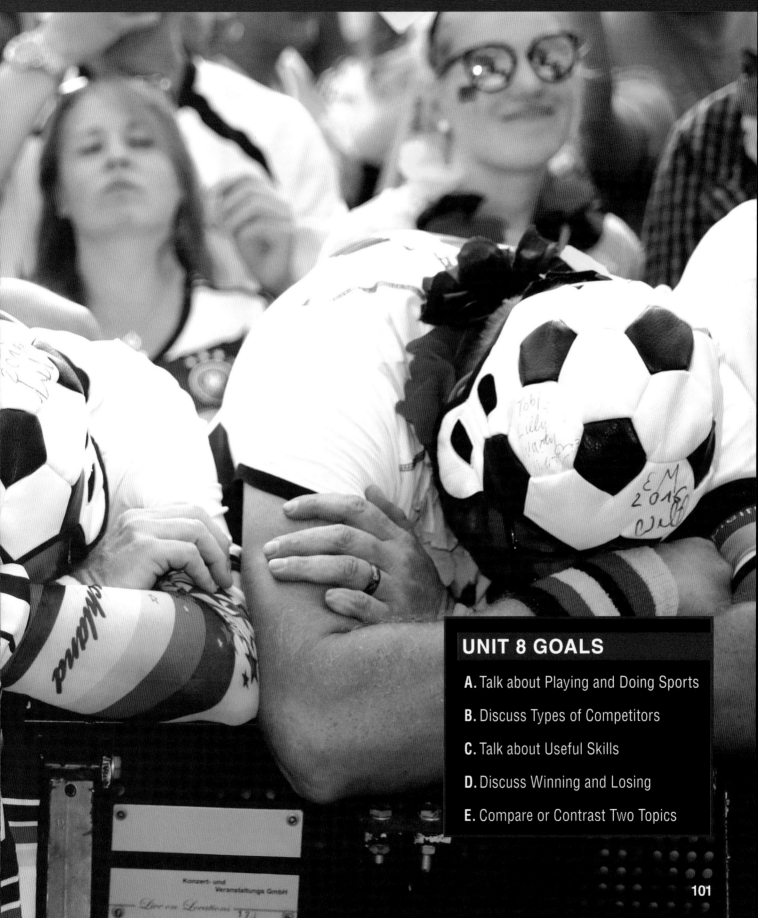

UNIT 8 GOALS

A. Talk about Playing and Doing Sports

B. Discuss Types of Competitors

C. Talk about Useful Skills

D. Discuss Winning and Losing

E. Compare or Contrast Two Topics

GOAL Talk about Playing and Doing Sports

Vocabulary

A Read the text. Complete each definition with a blue word.

The sports industry is one of the largest industries in the world. Billions of people enjoy it. For example, they might like playing tennis, or going skiing, or doing yoga. They buy equipment to do these activities in order to become fit and develop strong muscles.

However, the big money comes from professional sports. All over the world, people pay to watch sporting events like the Olympics. Part of the reason why sports are popular is because of the drama. In order for a competitor or team to win a game or a championship, another person or team must lose. Winning brings happiness, but failure brings disappointment.

Because sports are such big business, TV companies pay a lot of money to show them. In the US, for instance, the National Football League receives around $7.5 billion each year for TV rights. And in some sports, such as soccer, companies pay millions to put their name and logo on a team's uniform. Individual athletes get huge money, too. The very best players—the ones who conquer everyone else to become champions—can make many millions of dollars a year. Unfortunately, few people have the talent or skills to play at this level.

Team members of the HK Typhoon underwater hockey club practice playing in Hong Kong.

1. _____ are people who are good at sports and participate in them.

2. _____ is a situation in which a person loses or does not succeed.

3. _____ allow body parts to move.

4. A _____ is a group of teams that compete against each other regularly.

5. _____ are people or teams that win a competition.

6. A _____ is somebody who takes part in a sporting event and tries hard to win.

7. A _____ is a competition to find the best team or player.

8. Sports _____ are games, races, or other competitions that people attend.

9. _____ describes sports that are a business, or people who get paid to play.

10. To _____ something is to try hard until you succeed.

B Expand your vocabulary by learning the verb form of *champion*, *competitor*, and *failure*, and the adjective forms of *competitor* and *athlete*.

Grammar

Tag Questions

Use tag questions to check information or confirm an opinion. Add a tag to turn a statement into a *yes / no* question. If the main part of the sentence does not have an auxiliary verb, the question tag uses an appropriate form of *do*.	He's very competitive. → He's very competitive, **isn't he**? You like playing soccer. → You like playing soccer, **don't you**?
For positive statements, add a negative tag. For negative statements, add a positive tag.	They're very athletic, **aren't they**? I probably won't win, **will I**?
To avoid confusion, don't answer tag questions with just "Yes" or "No." Instead, answer with a full sentence.	A: You don't like golf, **do you**? B: Yes. B: Actually, yes, I do. C: No. C: No, you're right, I don't.
Use rising intonation with tag questions when you are not sure if the answer will be *yes* or *no*. Use falling intonation when you are sure (or fairly sure) what the answer will be.	They can't win, **can they**? (unsure) He's playing well, **isn't he**? (sure)

C Circle the correct tags. In pairs, take turns asking and answering the questions.

1. You were a professional tennis player, *have / haven't / were / weren't* you?

2. You have never won a world championship, *are / aren't / have / haven't* you?

3. You enjoy watching sports events on TV, *can / can't / do / don't* you?

4. Most athletes should have big muscles, *will / won't / should / shouldn't* they?

5. Sports leagues can make a lot of money, *do / don't / can / can't* they?

 GOAL CHECK Talk about Playing and Doing Sports

Complete the steps.

1. Read the information in the box about using *play*, *go*, and *do*, and underline examples in **A**.

2. Complete the tag questions below in your own words.

3. Interview other students using your questions. Count how many positive and negative answers you get for each question.

   - You won't go _____ later, will you?
   - You don't do _____, do you?
   - You like playing _____?
   - You know how to play _____?
   - You're pretty good at _____?

> Use **play** for ball sports (e.g., play soccer) or some types of games (e.g., play video games). Use **go** for most *-ing* activities (e.g., go swimming). Use **do** for individual activities that have no ball (e.g., do karate).

GOAL Discuss Types of Competitors

Listening

A You will hear a successful athlete being interviewed on a sports radio station. Before listening, discuss these questions in small groups.

1. Is the interviewer more likely to be a man or a woman? Why?

2. Is the successful athlete probably a man or a woman? Why?

B 🎧 38 Listen to the interview. Check your answers in **A**.

C 🎧 38 Listen to the interview again. Who makes each point? Check (✓) the correct box.

1. In sports, men are generally faster and stronger than women. ☐ interviewer ☐ athlete

2. Men are sometimes faster than women, but they are not stronger. ☐ interviewer ☐ athlete

3. Coaches support female athletes less than they support male ones. ☐ interviewer ☐ athlete

4. People expect female athletes to stop doing sports after they marry. ☐ interviewer ☐ athlete

5. Female athletes compete against society as well as other athletes. ☐ interviewer ☐ athlete

6. Life is more challenging for women who are professional athletes. ☐ interviewer ☐ athlete

A boxer trains in Ankara, Turkey.

D In groups, discuss the opinions from **C**. Decide and write if each opinion is often *true*, *sometimes true*, or *rarely true*. Then, share your views with another group and explain why you assigned each opinion to that category.

True	Sometimes True	Rarely True

PRONUNCIATION: Use Intonation and Emphasis to Express Attitude

To express attitude or an opinion about something, you can use intonation and / or emphasis.

Really?   (rising intonation can suggest that you are surprised)

REALLY? (falling intonation and emphasis can suggest that you are angry)

Really?   (falling intonation can suggest that you don't believe someone)

E 🎧 39 Listen to some excerpts from the interview. How does the speaker feel?

1. ☐ pleased   ☐ surprised   ☐ irritated
2. ☐ proud   ☐ happy   ☐ excited
3. ☐ doubtful   ☐ apologetic   ☐ confident
4. ☐ worried   ☐ confused   ☐ impressed

WORD FOCUS

If a person is **apologetic**, he or she is sorry about something.

F In groups, take turns choosing one of the attitudes in **E** and saying something about competition or competitors using intonation or emphasis to show it. Can your classmates guess what attitude you chose?

✓ **GOAL CHECK** Discuss Types of Competitors

Discuss each question below in a different group. Support your opinions with reasons, details, and examples. Use intonation and emphasis to express your attitude.

1. How true is it that tall people are better at basketball than short people?
2. How true is it that men are better at playing video games than women?
3. How true is it that young people are better at sports than older people?
4. How true is it that the best athletes make the most money from sports?

C GOAL Talk about Useful Skills

Language Expansion: Sports Skills

balance
commitment
communication
leadership
speed
stamina
strength
teamwork

A Complete each definition below with a word from the box. Then decide whether they are *physical skills* or *mental skills*.

1. _____ is guiding a group of people or an organization.

2. _____ is having enough energy to move or run for a long time.

3. _____ is having powerful muscles and being physically strong.

4. _____ is how fast something moves, or the ability to move quickly.

5. _____ is not falling over while you are running or jumping.

6. _____ is talking in a way that helps others understand you.

7. _____ is working hard at something in order to be successful.

8. _____ is working with others, including coaches, to be successful.

WORD FOCUS

A **coach** helps athletes to improve their skills.

A **captain** leads a sports team.

B In small groups, make a list of other physical or mental skills that are useful for sports.

SPEAKING STRATEGY

Use **which** to sound more formal when you are adding additional information.

C 🎧 40 In pairs, complete the conversation with words from **A**. Then listen and check your answers.

Coach: I'd like you to be our new team captain, Sam. What do you say?

Sam: Me? Why? There are other players who are better. For example, I don't have much (1) _____ or (2) _____. Alex and Chris are both faster than me, and there are several people who are stronger than me.

Coach: Well, perhaps, but you have excellent (3) _____. Nobody can keep running and running like you do. Your balance and teamwork are good too.

Sam: I guess, but...

Coach: Plus, you have several skills which are really important for a captain. For one thing, your (4) _____ is very good. Everybody trusts you to make the right decisions. Moreover, your (5) _____ skills are great, too. When you give advice, people listen. Finally, and most importantly, there's nobody on the team with as much (6) _____ to winning as you. In fact, I've never coached anyone that is such a competitor.

Sam: Wow! Thanks, Coach. I really appreciate it. And yes, I'd love to be captain!

Grammar

Adjective Clauses 2

Look at these two sentences:

There are other players. They are better.

Notice how the second sentence gives more information about the noun (*players*) in the first sentence. This is because it explains which "players" the speaker is talking about.

In cases like this, use an adjective clause starting with a relative pronoun, like *who, which,* or *that*, to join the sentences. This will make your speaking and writing seem more natural:

*There are other players **who** are better.*

D In pairs, complete the tasks.

1. Underline the adjective clauses in the conversation in **C**. Discuss if another word like *who, which,* or *that* would be possible in each case.

2. Practice the conversation in **C**. Switch roles and practice again.

E Complete these sentences in your own words. Then, in groups, share your sentences and take turns asking questions to find out more.

1. I have a good friend who _____.

2. I like doing activities that _____.

3. I used to enjoy doing things which _____.

4. I dislike playing sports with people that _____.

> What's your friend's name?

> Why do you like these kinds of activities?

 GOAL CHECK Talk about Useful Skills

1. Think of two activities. They can be sports or things you do in your daily life. Make a list of skills that are useful for each activity.

2. In small groups, take turns sharing your lists. Can your team members guess which activities you have in mind?

3. After you have all shared your lists, discuss which skills are the most useful in your daily life, and why.

> My list of skills includes strength, speed,...

> Is playing soccer the activity you have in mind?

> Not soccer, no, but it's a similar sport.

Surfers need physical strength and balance to be successful at their sport.

D GOAL Discuss Winning and Losing

Reading

A **MY WORLD** In pairs, share a time when you won something. What happened? How do you feel about it now?

B Read the title of the text. In small groups, discuss how losing could mean winning.

C Read the text. Complete each statement with a phrase from the box.

about losing the game	across North America	from 2012 to 2015
in the draft	to other teams	within the rules

1. England's players probably did not feel too disappointed _____.

2. Tanking is something that happens in sports leagues _____.

3. A team that loses many games can get great players _____.

4. The Chicago Cubs baseball team lost many games _____.

5. Some fans do not like their team tanking, but doing it is _____.

6. One way for teams to tank is for owners to trade players _____.

D In pairs, discuss what parts of the text most surprised you and interested you.

✓ GOAL CHECK

In small groups, read and discuss the quotations about winning and losing. What does each quotation mean? How true do you think each quotation is?

1. "A champion is afraid of losing. Everyone else is afraid of winning."—Billie Jean King, former tennis player

2. "Losing feels worse than winning feels good."—Vin Scully, former baseball broadcaster

3. "There are more important things in life than winning or losing a game."—Lionel Messi, soccer player

4. "Winning is a habit. Unfortunately, so is losing." —Vince Lombardi, former American football coach

5. "Winning is great, sure, but if you are really going to do something in life, the secret is learning how to lose." —Wilma Rudolph, former sprinter

When Losing Means Winning

In sports, we expect that athletes and teams will play to win. In most cases, this is true. In unusual cases, however, trying to lose may be better. Take the soccer World Cup in 2018. England had to play Belgium. The team that won would stay in the competition, but would play great teams like Brazil or France in future games. The team that lost would also stay in the competition, but would play less famous teams like Denmark or Sweden. In other words, the losing team would have easier games and have more chances to win the whole competition. In the end, Belgium won the game. But for England, losing did not feel like failure: The team easily reached the semi-final, the country's best result in almost 30 years.

In some North American sports leagues, losing can also mean winning. However, unlike the example of England and Belgium, in these leagues, a team must lose many games in some years in order to win in future years. The reason for this strange situation is something called a *draft*. Each year, every team gets a chance to add the best young players from around the country. Teams with very bad records get the first chances to pick players, and teams with good records get the last chances. So losing a lot gives a team a good chance to draft a great young player.

Why is drafting players important? Well, a team that can add several top players can improve a lot very quickly. The team might even become good enough to win a championship. That sounds surprising, but it has happened many times. In baseball, for example, the Chicago Cubs and Houston Astros were bad teams for years. They lost game after game. Losing let both teams draft many young players. These new players were very good. They were so good, in fact, that the Cubs won the baseball World Series in 2016. Then, just one year later, the Astros won it.

When a team tries to lose often in order to draft great players, it is called "tanking." This is sometimes unpopular with fans, but it is not against the rules. Still, how do teams actually do it? Trading players is a common way. A tanking team can trade its best players to other teams. In return, it can get extra draft picks. This has two benefits. First, the tanking team is more likely to lose because it no longer has its best players. Second, when the draft happens, the team can use the extra picks to get even more great young players. In this way, a tanking team can go from worst to first in just a few years.

GOAL Compare or Contrast Two Topics

Communication

A Make a list of six sports you know. Rank them in order of how much you like them. Then, complete the tasks.

1. Find someone whose top sport is the same as yours. Discuss why you like this sport so much.

2. Find someone whose least favorite sport is the same as yours. Discuss what you dislike about this sport and why.

3. Find someone whose list includes a sport that you don't know much about. Ask questions about the rules of this sport.

B In groups, share your lists of sports from **A**. Then, discuss the questions. Support your opinions with reasons, details, and examples.

1. Which sports on your list are interesting to play, and which are interesting to watch?

2. Which sports are better for taller people, and which are more suitable for shorter people?

3. Which sports on your list are the easiest to play, and which are the hardest?

Writing

WRITING SKILL: Comparing and Contrasting

One common type of writing task is to compare and contrast two subjects, such as the benefits of doing team sports or individual sports. You can organize this type of writing in two ways.

Organize by Point	**Organize by Subject**
You need two or three paragraphs—one for each point you will focus on. Each paragraph: • explains how one point relates to subject one. • explains how this the same point relates to subject two.	You need two paragraphs—one for each of the subjects you are comparing. Each paragraph explains how a few points (usually no more than three) relate to one of your two subjects.

Conclusion
In a separate, final paragraph, you need to add a conclusion that states which of the two subjects you think is better.

C Read the compare and contrast text. In pairs, discuss how it is organized: by point or by subject. Then, work together to rewrite the piece using the other kind of organization.

Doing Team Sports or Individual Sports

Playing sports is often a good way to make friends. People who play team sports can become good friends with the other players on their team. For example, they can become friendly when they practice or play games, or if they go out together after practice. In contrast, people who play individual sports have fewer opportunities to make friends because they play alone.

Playing sports is also a good way to become fit and healthy. For most team sports, players need to run, jump, throw or hit a ball, and so on. These kinds of activities are good for people's bodies. In terms of health and fitness, individual sports are about the same as team sports. Players usually do the same things: running, jumping, and throwing or hitting a ball.

In conclusion, both team sports and individual sports have good points. On the whole, though, I think team sports are the better option for most people because of the social benefits they offer.

D Read the text again. In pairs, underline examples of compare and contrast language. Then, make a list of other useful language for comparing and contrasting. Share your list with another pair.

E Choose one of these topics and write a compare and contrast text. When you have finished, share your texts in pairs. Discuss which topics you chose, how you chose to organize your responses, and which compare and contrast expressions you used.

  a. Compare and contrast two sports that are popular in your country.

  b. Compare and contrast watching sports with playing sports.

  c. Compare and contrast the benefits of two ways of doing something.

  d. Compare and contrast two kinds of entertainment that many people like.

 GOAL CHECK Compare or Contrast Two Topics

In groups, discuss which will be more popular in the future, and why: traditional sports or eSports (video game competitions in which many players take part). When you have finished, share your ideas and reasons with the class.

VIDEO JOURNAL

TED TALKS

WHAT I LEARNED WHEN I CONQUERED THE WORLD'S TOUGHEST TRIATHLON

A You are going to watch a TED Talk by Minda Dentler about taking part in a triathlon. Discuss these questions in groups.

1. Read Dentler's **idea worth spreading**. What do you think it means?

2. Do you think Dentler's biggest challenge was physical or mental? Why?

B Watch the first part of the TED Talk and take notes. Then, in pairs, complete the information with numbers from the box.

2.4	10.5	15	17	26.2
28	34	98	112	140.6

1. The climb to the town of Hawi is a distance of [   ] miles.

2. The temperature on race day was [   ] degrees Fahrenheit.

3. Dentler's age was [   ] when she first competed in an Ironman competition.

4. The distance of the swim in the Kona Ironman is [   ] miles.

5. After swimming, Minda had to hand cycle another [   ] miles.

6. Finally, she had to run a marathon, a distance of [   ] miles.

7. In total, Dentler had to travel [   ] miles using just her arms.

8. She had to complete the total distance in [   ] hours or less.

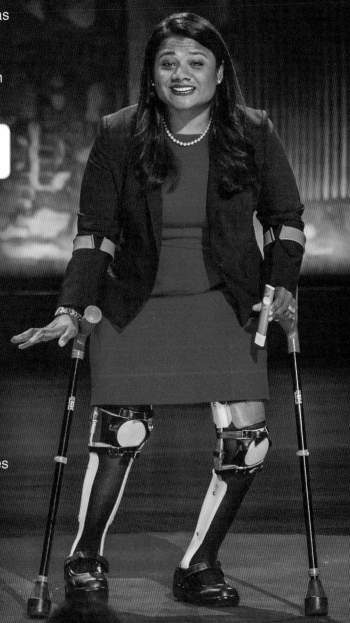

C Predict the order in which Dentler discusses these things in the rest of the talk. Then, watch once or twice to confirm your answers.

	Her experiences dealing with polio when she was a child
	Her feelings at the end of her second Ironman competition
	How she pushed herself to complete the bike ride in time
	Some details about how much of a problem polio still is
	The people who helped her get to the top of Palani Hill
1	What she felt about not completing her first Ironman event
	Why she wants to get rid of polio and how she plans to do it

D Complete these tasks in small groups. Support your views with reasons and examples.

1. Discuss how Dentler's talk made you feel.

2. Discuss whether you would recommend her talk to somebody who has not seen it.

3. Write a two-sentence summary of her talk. Share it with another group. Discuss the strengths of each summary.

E In different small groups, discuss these questions. Support your views.

1. When she took part in the Ironman events, who or what was Dentler competing against?

2. Make a list of five of the greatest athletes you know. In what ways is Dentler like these people? In what ways is she different?

F Dentler ends her talk by asking, "What is your Ironman?" Prepare, and then practice and deliver a 90-second response to this question. In your response:

• say what you think her question means.

• give your own answer to this question.

• say why you would answer it in this way.

MINDA DENTLER
Record Setting Triathlete,
Polio Survivor

Minda Dentler's **idea worth spreading** is that winning a competition is not about a medal, but about the inspiration to conquer fear of failure and achieve one's goals.

Danger

A great white shark follows a marine biologist in a kayak off the coast of South Africa.

Look at the photo and answer the questions:

1 What is the most dangerous thing in the photo?

2 How often do you think about danger?

GOAL Ask about Personal Fears

Vocabulary

A Read the text. Tell a partner which of the phobias you have, if any.

People stand on a glass skywalk at Tianmen Mountain in Zhangjiajie, China.

A phobia is a strong fear of something, even if that thing is not likely to cause harm. As the definition suggests, people with specific phobias fear a particular thing. For example, a person with claustrophobia is scared of being in small spaces. In contrast, those with social phobias worry about the reaction of other people in certain situations. Glossophobia, the fear of speaking in public, is a common example.

The cause of social phobias is not clear, but scientists think there are several reasons for specific phobias. In some cases, they develop because of a real danger. For instance, if a child has an allergy to bee stings, she might develop a phobia of bees. This happens because she knows they are a risk to her safety. In other cases, bad past experiences can cause phobias. A man who has an illness after eating mushrooms might develop fungophobia, for example. Finally, a child who hates injections might develop a phobia of sharp objects that can cause injury.

Specific phobias are rarely a serious problem. A person with a snake phobia may have a small accident running away from a cobra, but may never be actually bitten by one. In contrast, social phobias can be more serious. In the worst cases, people avoid most social situations and hardly ever go out.

WORD FOCUS

A doctor might give you an **injection** by putting a sharp needle into your arm.

B Complete each sentence with a word in blue from **A**.

1. A _____ is something that could cause problems or danger.

2. A person's _____ to something is what he or she says or does because of it.

3. An _____ is a sudden event that often leaves people injured.

4. An _____ is a disease or physical condition that makes people feel unwell.

5. If a person has an _____ to a food, eating it can make him or her very sick.

6. If a person has an _____, part of his or her body is hurt.

7. People usually _____ situations that they do not like.

8. Something that does _____ causes injury or damage.

9. Something that is _____ has an edge or point that could easily cut somebody.

10. _____ is the condition of being safe and not in any danger.

C Expand your vocabulary by learning the verb form of *harm*, *injury*, and *reaction*, and the adjective form of *accident*, *allergy*, *illness*, *injury*, *risk*, and *safety*.

Grammar

Negative Questions	
Negative questions are *yes / no* questions that start with either the negative form of *are*, *do*, or *have* or the negative form of a modal like *can*, *will*, *could*, *should*, or *would*.	**Weren't** you really scared? **Hasn't** his illness improved? **Won't** it be too dangerous? **Shouldn't** you see a doctor?
We use negative questions in several situations. Three of them are relatively common: **1.** To confirm something you already know or think **2.** To show that you are surprised or annoyed **3.** To give advice or make a suggestion indirectly	**1. Don't** you have a fear of spiders? (I think you *do* have this fear.) **2. Can't** you be more careful? (I am annoyed by your behavior.) **3. Shouldn't** you call her first? (My advice is to call her first.)

D In pairs, write negative questions in response to these situations. Then, make up new situations and create negative questions in response.

> Don't you have a phobia of snakes?

> Yes, I do.

1. A friend drops a glass but does not pick up the sharp pieces.

_____

2. A coworker says, "Let's leave work early and go to a movie!"

_____

3. A family member is driving a car but is not wearing a seatbelt.

_____

4. It is two o'clock in the morning but your neighbor is playing loud music.

_____

5. A stranger falls in the street and seems to have a leg injury.

_____

 GOAL CHECK Ask about Personal Fears

In pairs, complete the steps.

1. Think of a phobia each of you have. Do not say it out loud.

2. Take turns asking negative questions to find out each other's fears.

3. When you know your partner's fear, repeat steps 1 and 2 with a different partner.

GOAL Discuss Dangerous Jobs

Listening

A Read the definition. Then, in groups, discuss the questions.

> **stunt person** (noun) /ˈstənt-ˌpər-sᵊn/
> a person whose job is to do dangerous things for a movie or
> television show so that the actors can stay safe

1. What type of person is likely to work as a stunt person? Why do you think people choose this job?

2. Do you think a stunt person's job is really dangerous, or does it just look dangerous?

B 🎧 42 Listen to a stunt person talk about her job. Number these questions in the order she talks about them.

- _____ Are famous actors nice people?

- _____ Do you get paid a lot of money?

- _____ How did you get into stunt work?

- _____ Is being a stunt person dangerous?

C 🎧 43 Listen to some excerpts from the talk. Circle the correct answers.

1. What does the woman imply when she says, "At least not while working as a stunt person"?

   a. She broke a bone before becoming a stunt person.

   b. She thinks that she will break a bone in the future.

2. What does she imply when she says, "There are some actors I'll never work with again"?

   a. Some actors behave badly.

   b. Some actors have retired.

3. What does she imply when she says, "A lot of my friends in the industry tell similar stories"?

   a. Many stunt people want to become actors or writers.

   b. Her reason for becoming a stunt person is common.

4. Why does she say this: "I'll be an old lady before I've earned even a single million"?

   a. To emphasize that she does not make much money

   b. To imply that older stunt people make more money

5. What does she suggest when she says, "I'm 42 now, so I should think about life after stunt work"?

   a. Older stunt people have more accidents.

   b. The majority of stunt people are young.

D Discuss these questions in groups.

1. What adjectives describe your reaction to the talk?

2. Would you like to work as a stunt person? Why?

3. If you could ask this stunt person a question, what would you ask her?

PRONUNCIATION: Consonant Clusters

Some English words have clusters, or groups, of consonants next to each other (Consonants include every letter except the vowels: *a, e, i, o, u,* and sometimes *y*). Longer clusters can be hard to pronounce, especially at the end of words. For example, the cluster-*sks* in *risks*. To make pronouncing clusters easier, you might notice that some speakers may drop one of the consonant sounds without realizing it, or may say it very quickly.

E 🎧 44 Look at these words from the talk. Say all three pronunciations of the word in bold. Which one sounds the most natural? Then listen and check (✓) the pronunciation that you hear.

1. With many **risks**   ☐ risks   ☐ riss   ☐ riks

2. A few **months** ago   ☐ months   ☐ moths   ☐ mons

3. Speed and **strength**   ☐ strength   ☐ strenth   ☐ stregth

4. A friend **asked**   ☐ askt   ☐ ast   ☐ akt

✓ GOAL CHECK Discuss Dangerous Jobs

During her talk, the stunt person said the three most dangerous jobs "involve cutting down trees, catching fish, and flying airplanes." Discuss these questions in a group.

1. What are some other jobs that can be very dangerous?

2. What is a dangerous job you would *never* do? What is one you *might* do? Why?

3. What are some positive things about doing a dangerous job?

4. In the future, robots might do all dangerous jobs. Would this be good or bad? Why?

Skydivers train for their free fall jumps.

GOAL Talk about Common Injuries

Language Expansion: Common Injuries

Our world is usually safe, but some common activities can be dangerous. For example, doing sports can lead to injuries. If a hard ball hits a person, it can cause a bruise. The skin will change color and be painful to touch. If a person who is running falls down, she may get a scrape on her knee or elbow where the skin is rubbed off. And if the person twists an ankle, elbow, or other joint, he may have a sprain. Cooking is another activity that can be dangerous. A person may get a cut if he is not careful when using a knife. And touching a hot pan can cause a burn. Finally, being in an accident often causes an injury. If a person falls off his bike, for example, it is possible that he will have a break, or fracture, in a bone.

WORD FOCUS

A **joint** is a place in the body where two bones connect, such as the knee.

A Read the text about common injuries. Then, complete the tasks in groups.

1. In your notebooks, write a definition of each word in blue. Use a dictionary if you wish.

2. Rewrite each sentence from the text that contains a blue word. Use the verb form of the word.

3. Discuss some activities that people often do at home, at work, and at the park that can lead to common injuries. When you have finished, join another group and compare ideas.

Conversation

REAL LANGUAGE

We describe somebody who often has accidents as being **accident-prone**.

B 🎧 45 In pairs, predict which body parts Greg injured. Then, listen to check your answers.

Tina: Oh my gosh! What happened to you, Greg?

Greg: When I was biking to work two days ago, I had an accident. I cut my (1) _____ and scraped and bruised my (2) _____.

Tina: You should always wear a helmet when you ride. Head injuries can be very serious.

SPEAKING STRATEGY

Use **Don't you know** … in a negative question to show that you are surprised or annoyed by something someone did.

Greg: I also sprained my (3) _____ while I was jogging yesterday. That's why I'm limping.

Tina: But it snowed yesterday. Don't you know that you shouldn't run if the streets are icy?

Greg: Oh, and as I was making breakfast this morning, I accidentally burned my (4) _____.

Tina: You're so accident-prone! Always check if something is hot before touching it, OK?

Grammar

Adverbials of Time	
Adverbials are clauses or phrases that give more information about the main verb of a sentence. Adverbials of time explain *when* something happened.	Greg broke his leg **as he was playing football**. She sprained her knee **just before the race**.
Clauses include a <u>time conjunction</u> like *while* or *when* plus a subject and verb.	**When she fell over**, the girl bruised her leg.
Phrases include a <u>time preposition</u> like *after* or *before* and an object instead of a subject and verb.	The boy cried **after scraping his knee**.
Use a comma after a time adverbial when it comes before the main clause.	**As soon as he burned his leg,** he called 911. He called 911 **as soon as he burned his leg**.

C Read the grammar information. Then, in pairs, complete the tasks.

1. Write the adverbials of time you find in the conversation in **B**.

_____

_____

_____

_____

_____

2. Take turns practicing each role in the conversation.

3. Change the conversation so that Greg has different accidents and Tina makes different comments. Practice your new conversation in front of another pair of students.

GOAL CHECK Talk about Common Injuries

Complete the steps in small groups.

1. Find a minor injury that *all* of you have experienced. For example, maybe all of you have fractured a bone or sprained a joint.

2. Prepare and practice a talk. You should say what injury all of you have experienced and when you experienced it. You should also give advice about how to avoid this kind of injury as well as how to treat the injury after it has happened.

3. Deliver your talk in front of the class. Make sure each person in your group speaks.

4. Discuss which injury was the most common in the class. Also discuss which advice for avoiding and treating injuries was the most useful.

> I burned my hand when I was a child. Anyone else?

> Me, too. It was so painful!

> I haven't burned my hand, but I burned my leg once.

D GOAL Discuss the Benefits of Danger

Reading

A Discuss the questions in small groups.

1. Look at the photo. Did you enjoy doing this activity when you were a child? Why?

2. The title of the article is a question. How would you answer it?

B Read the text. Would the author probably agree with statements 1–5? Write *Yes* or *No* if the writer's view is obvious or *Unsure* if it is not clear.

1. _____ The world is less dangerous now than it was 50 years ago.

2. _____ Children would have fewer allergies if they ate more eggs.

3. _____ Most parents these days can be described as "free range."

4. _____ Gever Tulley's book was written for parents, not for children.

5. _____ Aristotle said, "everything in moderation" for children only.

C Read the comments about the text. Then, complete the steps.

Are you kidding? This is a terrible post. The police should arrest all "free range" parents. ____

Great post. I think a little danger is a good thing not just for kids, but for adults, too. ____

I used to agree that too much safety was bad, but having kids changes you. Now I feel that nothing's more important than keeping your children safe. ____

1. Put the comments in order from the one you agree with most to the one you agree with least.

2. Find a classmate who put them in a different order. Discuss why you disagree.

✓ GOAL CHECK

In groups, come up with five dangerous activities that could benefit children (or adults). Share your activities with the class and explain why doing them might bring benefits. Which of the activities have you done? Which would you like to do?

Is Too Much Safety a Risk?

For most people, life today is safer than it was 1,000, 100, or even 10 years ago. However, the world still has some dangers, so most parents spend time and money keeping their children as safe as possible. They buy them helmets to wear when riding a bike. They keep them away from things that could cause injury. They avoid letting their children be in any kind of harm. These actions seem good, but some people argue that too much safety may actually be bad.

These people say that children cannot learn how to stay safe if they are never in dangerous situations. They think children will not know how to deal with dangers or problems because they do not have experience doing these things. They also argue that children

learn when they do dangerous things. For example, they learn to take responsibility for themselves and their actions. They also learn to control things and be independent. And, as children often have little control or independence, those can be powerful feelings.

According to the "**hygiene** theory," keeping children too safe may also cause health issues. These days, more and more children have allergies to foods like nuts or eggs. A possible reason is that people are protecting their children too much. They do not let their children play with other children who have an illness, or they stop their children from playing outside. As a result, their children's bodies are not used to **germs** or dirt. And when these children eat a food that is normal, their bodies may have a dangerously strong reaction.

So, what should parents do? Some people choose to be "free range" parents who give their children freedom to do things on their own. For

example, they may let their children walk to a park and play there alone. They feel that this kind of freedom will teach their children important skills. But some parents worry that "free range" parenting is too much. For these parents, there are books and websites that suggest some dangerous activities children can do with an adult to help them. One of the most famous books is by Gever Tulley. His book is called *50 Dangerous Things (You Should Let Your Children Do)*. Examples of these dangerous things include letting children drive a car or walk home from school alone.

So, is it true that too much safety can be dangerous? Perhaps the answer comes from Aristotle, the famous Greek writer. He wrote that doing "everything in **moderation**" leads to the best life.

hygiene keeping your body, home, or workplace clean
germs small living things that can cause an illness
moderation neither too much nor too little of anything

GOAL Give Clear Instructions

A Complete the text with words from the box. Some words are extra.

backyard
dining room
garage
kitchen
living room
playroom

We think of our homes as safe places where we can relax. This is often true, but it's also true that accidents can happen at home. For example, fires can start in the (1) _____, and people can burn or cut themselves while cooking. In the (2) _____, children can be injured when jumping on a chair or sofa, or if a television set falls on them. In the (3) _____, cars can be dangerous, of course, and many people store sharp tools or objects there, too. And outside in the (4) _____, barbecues or play equipment can harm people if they're not used correctly.

Communication

B In pairs, complete the tasks.

1. Compare your answers from **A**. What clues helped you choose each answer?

2. Discuss other accidents that could happen in the rooms mentioned in **A**.

3. Discuss what accidents might happen in the room in the photo below.

4. Decide which room you think is the most dangerous in a typical home. Explain why.

C Interview three students other than your partner in **B**. Then, share what you learned with a new partner. Compare answers with your answer to question 4 in **B**.

Name	In which room did you have your worst accident at home?

COMMUNICATION SKILL: Giving Instructions

When you need to explain how to do or use something, you can give instructions. Here is some advice for giving clear, effective instructions:

- Giving instructions is like giving advice: you can use the imperative (base form of the main verb without subject), such as: **Follow** these instructions. The negative imperative is formed using do not (don't): **Don't run** through the hallway! You can also use modals such as must (not) or should (not).

- If your instructions must be followed in a certain order, it is a good idea to use clear sequence words such as first, second, third, next, after that, and so on.

- For very important instructions, such as safety instructions, use basic vocabulary and sentences so that no one will misunderstand. It may help to imagine that you are giving instructions to a child.

WORD FOCUS

A **crosswalk** is a place where the road is marked with black and white stripes to show where people should cross.

D Read the instructions. Then, in groups, complete the tasks.

Follow these instructions when you want to cross a road that does not have a crosswalk. First, find a place to cross where you can see the traffic in every direction. Next, wait by the side of the road. You should not stand too close to the edge. Then, look in all directions and listen. If you see or hear any traffic, wait until it has gone past. Finally, walk directly across the road without stopping.

1. Underline the imperatives and modals. One example has been done for you.
2. Circle the sequence words. One example has been done for you.
3. Discuss whether a child would easily understand these instructions.

Writing

E Write clear instructions about how to do *one* of these things safely. Use the instructions in **D** as a model.

- Cook food on a barbecue
- Clean up broken glass
- Cut wood with a saw
- Hike in the mountains

 GOAL CHECK Give Clear Instructions

Complete the steps.

1. In groups, share your instructions from **E** and discuss how to improve them.
2. Join a new group with people who wrote instructions about the same topic in **E**. Discuss how to combine your instructions so that you keep the best parts from each.
3. Present your combined instructions to the class.

VIDEO JOURNAL

AN EVERYDAY DANGER

A Read these quotations from the video you are going to watch. Then, in groups, predict who the speaker is and what problem the speaker is talking about.

"It is not a terminal illness that my child has, but it is an every day, every second, every moment risk."

"A lot of people think that they should be able to give their kids whatever foods they want ... What they don't understand is they're putting a child's life at risk."

"Immediately, within five minutes, my son was turning blue."

B Watch the first part of the video. Then, in pairs, discuss the questions in **A**. Did you correctly predict who the speaker is and the problem she is discussing?

C Watch the second part of the video. Complete the transcript with the words that Xaviar's mother says.

"Some people don't believe that food (1) _____ are real at all. A lot of people think that they should be able to give their kids whatever foods they want and send them off to (2) _____ with as much peanut butter, as much tree nuts ... What they don't understand is they're putting a child's life at risk. He could be on a (3) _____ and somebody could have a peanut butter and jelly (4) _____. This is why his being in school is so crazy, too, because they're using the same keyboards, they're opening the same (5) _____. It's the unknown that's really scary."

A visual representation of allergy testing at the University Hospital of Bordeaux, France.

126

D Watch the final part of the video. Match each statement to the person who says it.

a. Anastasia (Xaviar's mom)

b. Dr. Wood

c. Xaviar

1. _____ And then you put it back in the case ... call 911.

2. _____ I used to focus on the theories about why allergies happen.

3. _____ If we raise a child who is confident and happy with himself, hopefully he'll be just fine.

4. _____ It is very important to be ready for an accidental reaction.

5. _____ It's a combination of physical and emotional stuff we go through.

6. _____ The hygiene theory says that our environment is too clean.

E Xaviar's mother suggests that becoming an independent person will be dangerous for Xaviar. In groups, discuss these questions related to this point.

1. What dangers might Xaviar experience if he decides to travel the world?

2. What dangers might Xaviar experience if he decides to go to college?

3. Think of one more common life experience. What dangers might Xaviar face if he has this experience?

F In different groups, complete the tasks.

1. Xaviar's mother says that some people think food allergies are not real. Discuss why people might think this.

2. These days, people often use social media to spread a message. Discuss how you could use social media to persuade people that food allergies are real and that they should be more careful. When you have finished discussing, share your ideas with the class.

A visitor looks at the glowing rock walls and ceiling of Waitomo Caves in Waitomo, New Zealand.

UNIT 10 GOALS

A. Speculate about a Mystery

B. Discuss Why People Study the Past

C. Talk about Solving Mysteries

D. Discuss Theories and the Truth

E. Describe a Physical Object

129

GOAL Speculate about a Mystery

Vocabulary

A Read the text. Then, discuss your reaction to it with a partner.

The universe is huge. The number of stars in the universe is uncertain, but scientists think there may be as many as 400 billion in the part of the universe where Earth is located. Many of those stars may have planets, and many people believe that life may exist on at least some of them. So, some people wonder, "Where is everybody?" Many people have speculated about this mystery. They have come up with many theories to explain why we have not yet found any alien life. Here are three of them:

- One possibility is that life is very rare and that Earth is incredibly special; in other words, perhaps humans are alone in the universe.

- The universe is very ancient, so life could have existed on other worlds in the past but then died out before we could meet it.

- Another suggestion is that we do not have enough knowledge to recognize other life; aliens might have tried to contact us, but our technology was too basic to notice.

We have not discovered other life in our universe yet, but we continue to look for it. Perhaps we will get a message from another civilization soon. If that happens, there is no doubt it will have a very big impact on all of our lives.

B Circle the correct option to complete the definitions of the blue words in the text.

1. Something that is **uncertain** *may or may not be true* / *used to exist but no longer does*.

2. To **wonder** means to *read and learn* / *think and ask* about something.

3. To **speculate** means to think and discuss things that *are impossible* / *could happen*.

4. A **theory** is *an explanation for* / *a message about* something, but it may not be true.

5. A **possibility** is something that *people do not expect* / *might happen*.

The Allen Telescope Array in Hat Creek, California looks into space and searches for alien life.

6. Something **ancient** is very old or *happened a long time ago / has happened many times.*

7. A **suggestion** is an idea, plan, or action somebody *orders / recommends.*

8. **Knowledge** is *equipment that helps you learn / information you know* about a topic.

9. A **civilization** is a society *in which few people live / with a high level of development.*

10. To have **doubt** means to feel *unhappy about a situation / unsure if something is true.*

C Expand your vocabulary by learning the verb form of *doubt*, *knowledge*, and *suggestion*; the noun form of *speculate*, *uncertain*, and *wonder*; and the adjective form of *doubt*, *possibility*, and *theory*.

Grammar

Modals to Discuss the Past	
To talk about past possibilities or something that is uncertain about the past, use *could / may / might + have +* past participle.	It's a mystery why people stopped living in that city. One theory is that an earthquake **could / may / might have happened**.
To talk about something that is certain or almost certain about the past, use *must have +* past participle.	She has a lot of knowledge about dozens of ancient civilizations. She **must have studied** hard for many years.

D Read the grammar information. Then, in pairs, <u>underline</u> examples of modals that discuss the past in the text in **A**.

E Complete these sentences in your own words in your notebook. Then, in pairs, compare your answers. How similar are your sentences?

1. There was a flash of bright light under the water. It may have been _____.

2. Something moved very quickly through the sky. It might have been _____.

3. Some scientists discovered a mysterious signal. It could have been _____.

4. Many ancient species suddenly died out. The cause may have been _____.

F **MY WORLD** In pairs, talk about mysterious events you have experienced.

 GOAL CHECK Speculate about a Mystery

In groups, discuss these questions. Then, share your ideas with another group.

1. The text in **A** gives three theories that explain why we have not found alien life. What other explanations can you think of?

2. The same text says that finding other life "will have a very big impact" on us. Think of some ways this might change our lives.

GOAL Discuss Why People Study the Past

Listening

A Look at the list of famous people and choose two or three that you are most interested in learning more about. Then, find someone who chose different people and take turns giving reasons for your choices.

- Akhenaten, a pharaoh from Egypt
- Claudius, an emperor from Rome
- Edgar Allan Poe, a mystery writer
- Florence Nightingale, a nurse
- Mozart, a musician and composer
- Pericles, a politician from Greece

B 🎧 47 Listen to the conversation and choose the *two* correct answers for each question. Then, listen again to confirm your answers.

A statue of Akhenaten at the Egyptian Museum in Cairo, Egypt. He was the Pharaoh of Egypt from about 1353 to 1336 BC.

1. What do the speakers say about the book?
   a. It discusses people's deaths.
   b. It has just one chapter.
   c. It was published in Egypt.
   d. It was written by a doctor.

2. What do they say about Akhenaten?
   a. He did not look like most people.
   b. He had a lot of treasure.
   c. His child was also a pharaoh.
   d. His family faced many problems.

3. What do they say about Pericles?
   a. He died from a well-known disease.
   b. He died when he was 25 years old.
   c. He was a soldier and a politician.
   d. He was from the city of Athens.

4. What do they say about the people of Athens?
   a. A quarter of them died.
   b. They had long and unusual heads.
   c. Their disease caused vomiting.
   d. They were poisoned.

5. What do they say about Claudius?
   a. He had a fever and a heart attack.
   b. He may have been killed by somebody.
   c. He was a doctor before he was a ruler.
   d. He was one of the emperors of Rome.

C Discuss the questions in groups.

1. Would you like to read the book that the speakers discussed? Why?

2. Do you think it is likely that future scientists will solve any of the medical mysteries discussed in the book? Why?

PRONUNCIATION: Intonation for Lists

When saying a list of things, speakers often say *or* or *and* before the last item in the list to show that the list is about to finish. In these cases, the first items in the list will have a rising intonation, and the last item will have a falling intonation.

e.g., We don't know when he died, where he died, or how he died.

In some cases, the speaker may leave the list unfinished. In these cases, the last item in the list will also have a rising intonation.

e.g., We don't know when he died, where he died, how he died …

D 🎧 48 Listen to the information about intonation.

E 🎧 49 Listen to excerpts from the conversation in **B**. Circle the phrase that completes each list. Then, mark either rising or falling intonation.

1. …chapters about people like Christopher Columbus, Beethoven, *Mozart /
and Mozart*

2. …some leaders from the ancient world, including Egypt, Greece, *Rome /
and Rome*

3. …statues of Akhenaten show that he had an unusual face, body, *legs /
and legs*

4. …the disease had many nasty effects, including vomiting, headache, *fever /
and fever*

✓ **GOAL CHECK** Discuss Why People Study the Past

At the end of the conversation, the man says, "I wonder why people spend time studying the past." In groups, discuss some reasons why people do this.

GOAL Talk about Solving Mysteries

Language Expansion: Mystery Stories

A Complete the text with the correct singular or plural form of the words in **bold**.

- A **character** is a person in a story, a movie, or a play.

- A **clue** is a piece of information that helps solve a mystery.

- A **crime** is an action or activity that is against the law.

- A **deduction** is a specific idea that is based on logic and evidence.

- A **detective** is a person who tries to find clues to solve a crime.

- An **investigation** is the act of looking into a crime to solve it.

- **Evidence** is information that answers a question or solves a crime.

- **Proof** is information that shows something is definitely true.

In 2013, a mystery story called *The Cuckoo's Calling* was published. This book was apparently the first novel by a man called Robert Galbraith. Like most mysteries, the main (1) _____ in the book was a (2) _____ trying to solve a (3) _____. As part of his (4) _____, the detective looked for several (5) _____ to explain what had happened. After he found some (6) _____ about where and when the crime took place, he made a correct (7) _____ about who did it. People liked *The Cuckoo's Calling*, but it did not sell many copies at first. Soon after the book was published, some people said the writer was actually JK Rowling, the author of the Harry Potter stories. As soon as there was (8) _____ that this theory was correct, sales of the book increased by 4,000 percent.

Lello Bookstore, located in Porto, Portugal, inspired JK Rowling's writing of the Harry Potter books.

Grammar

Noun Clauses	
Noun clauses act as nouns in a sentence. They usually follow this pattern: *wh-* word + (subject) + verb + (object).	The detectives did not know **who did it**, but they did know **when and where it happened**.
Noun clauses can act as the subject of the sentence when they come before the verb.	**Where it took place** is a complete mystery. **Why she committed the crime** is unknown.
Noun clauses can act as an object when they come after a verb or a preposition.	I found clues that explained **why he did it**, but I have no ideas about **how it happened**.

B Read the information about noun clauses. Then, underline the noun clauses in the text in **A** and the conversation in **C**. Finally, compare your answers in pairs.

Conversation

C 🎧 50 In pairs, discuss which words from **A** best complete the conversation. Then, listen and check your answers.

José: Is that another book about how famous people died, Hanna?

Hanna: No, it's one of Agatha Christie's (1) _____ stories.

José: I don't know her. Is she famous?

Hanna: Definitely! She's one of the best-selling writers in history. Her most famous (2) _____ is a (3) _____ called Hercule Poirot, who is great at finding (4) _____ and other kinds of evidence.

José: Oh, it's a mystery story? I don't like those. I can never figure out who did it!

Hanna: Me, neither. And I always wonder how mystery writers come up with their ideas. Still, I love reading their books. Anyway, do you like any other kinds of books, José?

D Complete the tasks.

1. In pairs, take turns practicing each role in the conversation.

2. Find a different partner. Extend the conversation by adding two new lines each for both José and Hanna. Then, practice your extended conversation and present it to a different pair of students.

 GOAL CHECK Talk about Solving Mysteries

In groups, take turns talking about a mystery story you have read or a mystery movie or TV show you have seen. Explain what happened and how it happened, who did it, who solved the mystery, how they solved it, and so on.

WORD FOCUS

To **figure out** something means to understand it by thinking deeply about it.

SPEAKING STRATEGY

We use **Me, neither.** to agree with a negative statement of the previous speaker.

D GOAL Discuss Theories and the Truth

Reading

A Before reading, discuss these questions in groups. Then, read the first paragraph of the text and check your answers.

1. How far is the moon from Earth?

2. In what year did the first human step on the moon?

3. In what year did humans last visit the moon?

4. In total, how many humans have visited the moon?

B Read the text. Then, write **T** for *true* **F** for *false* or **NG** if the information is *not given*.

_____ 1. One quarter of people in the world think the moon landings were real.

_____ 2. Some people believe that winds blow on the surface of the moon.

_____ 3. The flag seems to be moving because of a problem with the equipment.

_____ 4. Astronauts on the moon could see stars, but their cameras could not.

_____ 5. Believing in conspiracy theories gives some people positive feelings.

C In groups, discuss what most interested you about the text, and why.

 GOAL CHECK

In groups, read the statements and discuss whether they describe a theory or the truth.

- Humans have landed on the moon several times.
- Aliens have already visited Earth.
- Human activity has changed Earth's climate.
- Technology companies spy on their customers.

Back to the Moon?

On July 16, 1969, the Apollo 11 rocket was launched into space. Sitting inside were Neil Armstrong, Buzz Aldrin, and Michael Collins. After a journey of around 238,855 miles and almost 110 hours, Armstrong and Aldrin became the first humans to step onto the moon and on the surface of another world. Over the next three years and five months, five more rockets traveled to the moon, and another 10 men stood on its surface. Or at least, this is what most people think.

Some people, however, have a different idea. Their belief is that humans never traveled to the moon. They feel that all of the evidence for the moon landings is fake. How many people believe this **conspiracy theory**? Some people may not want to admit they believe it, so the true number is in doubt. However, research suggests that up to one quarter of people in some countries think that humans have never visited the moon.

These people mention details that support their opinion. For example, they mention two points about videos and photographs from the moon's surface. First, they say these pictures show flags moving in the wind, but there is no wind on the moon. As a result, they argue that these pictures must have been taken on Earth. They also say that the pictures show no stars in the sky, so they could not have been taken by **astronauts** standing on the surface of the moon.

Do these points show that the moon landings did not happen? The answer is *no*. The piece of metal holding the top of the flag was damaged. It was not straight, so the flag could not hang straight down. As a result, it looks like it is moving. And no stars can be seen in the photographs because the sun is very bright on the moon. It is so bright, in fact, that although there were many stars in the sky, they did not show up in the pictures. So, there is no doubt about the moon landings: they did happen.

However, why so many people believe conspiracy theories is much more of a mystery. Research suggests there might be several reasons. First, life in our modern world can be difficult, and people may feel their lives are uncertain. This feeling can make people very uncomfortable. Conspiracy theories can give people a feeling of certainty, which is attractive. In addition, people who believe conspiracy theories may feel they have secret knowledge that other people do not have. This is also an attractive feeling.

NASA, the National Aeronautics and Space Administration, has said it will send humans to the moon again. The current plan is that this will happen within the next 10 years. Depending on what you think, the next trip to the moon will be either the seventh or the very first.

conspiracy theory a belief that an event did not happen the way most people think
astronaut a person who travels into space in a rocket

Super blue blood full moon over water

Communication

A Read the two descriptions and look at the photos. Then, in pairs, discuss which text describes which photo.

1. This object looks a little bit like a ball. It has about twelve sides that have holes in them and many small round things that stick out. It seems to be made of a golden metal. It is about 1.6–4.3 inches. It was made approximately in the second or third century AD in Europe. There is doubt about why and how people used it.

2. This object looks similar to an airplane. It has something that looks like eyes on the front, wings at the sides, and a tail at the back. It seems to be made of gold. It is roughly 2.3 inches long. It was made in South America almost 1,000 years ago. People are uncertain what it is and why it was made.

B In different groups, read the statements and discuss how likely each one is. Then, come up with other ideas.

- It could have been a children's toy.
- It may have been a piece of jewelry.
- It might have been a type of money.

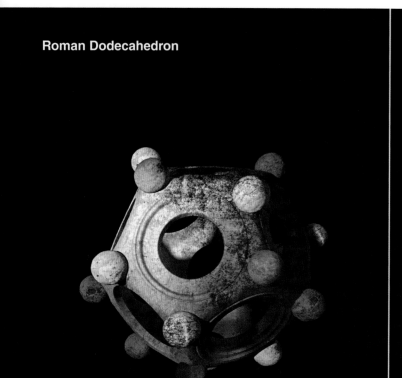

Roman Dodecahedron

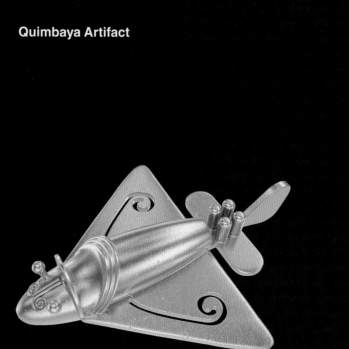

Quimbaya Artifact

COMMUNICATION SKILL: Describing an Object

When you describe an object, your goal is to help other people get a picture of it in their minds. To do this, you need to describe details such as the object's shape, size, weight, color, the material it's made from, and so on. If the object has special or unusual features, you should describe those as well.

If you are not certain about specific details or not sure how to describe a feature, use vague language in your description:

> It's *about* as big as a baseball. / It weighs *roughly* two pounds.
>
> *It seems to be* made of metal. / It's *a sort of* reddish-gold color.
>
> It has *something that looks like* eyes on the front. / *It has* little round things that stick out.

C Read the information in the box. Then, reread the texts in **A** and complete statements 3–6 with your own words.

1. The first sentences of both paragraphs *give a description of what the objects* look like
2. The second sentences *give specific details about the objects* _____.
3. The third sentences _____.
4. The fourth sentences _____.
5. The fifth sentences _____.
6. The final sentences _____.

Writing

D In pairs, choose an object in your classroom and write a description, but do not write the name of the object. Share your description with another pair of students. Can they recognize the object you described?

_____
_____
_____
_____
_____

 GOAL CHECK Describe a Physical Object

Think of an object you know well. Write a description of it that does not mention its name. Present your description to the class without using your notes. How many of your classmates recognized the object that you described?

VIDEO JOURNAL

FROM ANCIENT TO MODERN

A In groups, discuss what you know about ancient Mesopotamia, Egypt, Greece, and Rome. Then, discuss which culture is represented in the museum in the photograph.

B In the same groups, predict which two statements from a–h describe which ancient society.

1. Egypt _____ and _____
2. Greece _____ and _____
3. Rome _____ and _____
4. Mesopotamia _____ and _____

a. came up with the first system of writing

b. created the first democracy known to history

c. developed three different kinds of columns

d. had a big impact on the vocabulary of English

e. had a major influence on astronomy and the law

f. influenced languages like Spanish and Portuguese

g. introduced the 24-hour day and 365-day year

h. invented useful ways to bring water to fields

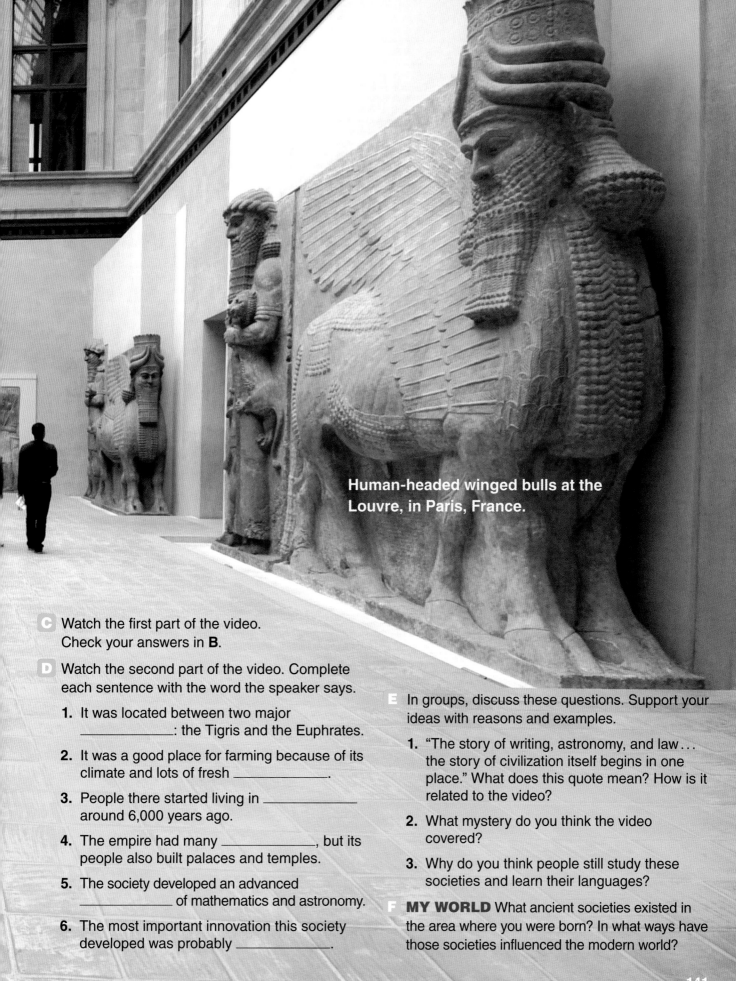

Human-headed winged bulls at the
Louvre, in Paris, France.

C Watch the first part of the video.
Check your answers in **B**.

D Watch the second part of the video. Complete
each sentence with the word the speaker says.

1. It was located between two major
_____: the Tigris and the Euphrates.

2. It was a good place for farming because of its
climate and lots of fresh _____.

3. People there started living in _____
around 6,000 years ago.

4. The empire had many _____, but its
people also built palaces and temples.

5. The society developed an advanced
_____ of mathematics and astronomy.

6. The most important innovation this society
developed was probably _____.

E In groups, discuss these questions. Support your
ideas with reasons and examples.

1. "The story of writing, astronomy, and law...
the story of civilization itself begins in one
place." What does this quote mean? How is it
related to the video?

2. What mystery do you think the video
covered?

3. Why do you think people still study these
societies and learn their languages?

F **MY WORLD** What ancient societies existed in
the area where you were born? In what ways have
those societies influenced the modern world?

Elementary school students in Hunan Province, China, learn science using virtual reality headsets.

UNIT 11 GOALS

A. Discuss Technology and Learning

B. Talk about Learning

C. Discuss Educational Choices

D. Talk about the Value of Play

E. Describe Problems and Solutions

A GOAL Discuss Technology and Learning

Vocabulary

A In pairs, discuss whether you need to add *a*, *an*, or nothing to complete the definitions. Then, compare your answers with another pair.

1. Something **academic** is connected to _____ education or studying.

2. To **achieve** something means to reach _____ goal after a lot of work.

3. To **attend** a school, a college, or _____ event means to go there.

4. To **concentrate** on _____ idea means to think about it very deeply.

5. **Confidence** is a feeling of _____ trust in somebody or something.

6. A **curriculum** is all of the topics studied as _____ part of a course.

7. A **degree** is _____ qualification you can get after studying at college.

8. An **expert** is a person with a lot of _____ knowledge about one topic.

9. **Motivation** is a strong feeling of _____ interest in doing something.

10. _____ **training** is teaching or learning skills that are useful for life or work.

B In pairs, expand your vocabulary by learning the verb form of *motivation* and *training*, the noun form of *academic*, *achieve*, *attend*, and *concentrate*, and the adjective form of *confidence*.

C In new pairs, complete the text with words from **A** or **B**. Check your answers with another pair.

> **WORD FOCUS**
> A **digital native** is a person who has used technology from a very early age.

Technology is now part of most aspects of our daily lives, including education. Educators are using computers, apps, and other kinds of technology more and more. The reason is that many students these days are digital natives. Some of them may find it easier to (1) _____ when learning from a screen than from a book. They may also feel more (2) _____ that they can trust what they are learning. These two things can help them (3) _____ greater success both inside and outside the classroom.

Technology brings another big benefit: it helps more people get a good education and high-quality (4) _____. It takes a lot of time and money to (5) _____ college or another (6) _____ institution. But with technology, people can study online for a college (7) _____ when it is convenient for them and for a much lower price. And in fact, technology makes it possible to get a great education for free. Some universities have uploaded the entire (8) _____ for some programs to the internet. So, people who are highly (9) _____ can study the material on their own and become an (10) _____ in a wide range of subjects from A to Z.

Grammar

Could Have, Should Have, and Would Have

Use *should have* + past participle to say that doing (or not doing) something was a good idea.	I **should have done** a degree online instead of attending a college in another state.
Use *could have* + past participle to say that something was possible.	With more motivation, he **could have achieved** a lot of success.
Use *would have* + past participle to say that something was likely to happen or somebody was likely to do something.	I think Tim **would have become** an expert in math, but he chose to concentrate on history.

D Read the grammar information. Then, circle examples of *could have*, *should have*, and *would have* in the sentences below.

1. I should have used **my phone to find a discount code**. I could have saved money.

2. I shouldn't have gone **running this morning**. I wouldn't have **hurt my leg.**

3. Both of my parents were great at **art**, so I could have been **a good artist**, too.

4. I should have texted you that **I was going to be late**. I'm sorry that I didn't.

5. I should have **studied harder in class**. I would have **passed the test easily**.

E In your notebook, copy the sentences from **D**, but rewrite the bold phrases in your own words. Then, share your sentences in pairs.

 GOAL CHECK Discuss Technology and Learning

In groups, complete the tasks.

1. Take turns saying what your school could have or should have done five years ago in order to use technology more effectively.

2. Share your positive and negative experiences of technology and learning. Discuss how you think technology will affect learning in the future.

A young student tests ideas at a new robotics center in Kiev, Ukraine.

B GOAL Talk about Learning

Listening

A In groups, discuss what each saying or quotation means and how much you agree with it.

- Practice makes perfect. (traditional saying)

- Play is our brain's favorite way of learning. (Diane Ackerman)

- Anyone who stops learning is old, whether at twenty or eighty. (Henry Ford)

- One child, one teacher, one book, and one pen can change the world. (Malala Yousafzai)

- It is not enough to learn how to ride; you must also learn how to fall. (traditional saying)

B **MY WORLD** In pairs, discuss any sayings about education or learning that you know or ones that you may have in your country.

C 🎧 52 Listen to part of a talk. Take notes. Then circle the correct option.

1. The speaker is probably a...

    a. former educator. **b.** university student.

2. The best title for this talk is...

    a. Research into Learning. **b.** Effective Skills for Teachers.

3. The speaker suggests that learning styles...

    a. are something that few people know about. **b.** may or may not be something people have.

A student takes a break from studying for an exam in Anhui, China.

4. The speaker explains that getting enough sleep...

    a. can help people exercise more often.

    b. improves how well people remember.

5. The speaker suggests that language learners...

    a. learn more if they repeat what they hear.

    b. may benefit from learning while working out.

6. According to the speaker, effective practice...

    a. can be done just once or twice but for a long time.

    b. should be done frequently but for short periods.

PRONUNCIATION: Enunciation

Enunciation is the act of speaking clearly. Listen to this sentence twice: once spoken normally, and once enunciated clearly.

They should have spent more time studying for their exams.

Notice how the words were clearer the second time because the speaker:

- said the beginning and end of each word clearly.
- paused slightly after each thought group.

When you enunciate well, people will understand what you are saying more easily. Research suggests they may better remember what you said, too. Learning how to enunciate can help you communicate more effectively in English and / or achieve a higher score on a speaking test.

D 🎧 53 Read and listen to the information in the box.

E 🎧 54 Listen to the sentences. Check (✓) the ones that the speaker enunciates well. Then, in pairs, take turns enunciating all of the sentences.

1. He was planning to attend a training course next week. _____

2. I would have done better if I had felt more confident. _____

3. She could have gotten a degree from a great school. _____

4. They were going to talk to an expert about the topic. _____

5. We should have concentrated harder in grammar class. _____

 GOAL CHECK Talk about Learning

In groups, discuss these questions.

1. What is the most interesting thing about learning that the speaker in **C** discussed? Why?

2. Will you change how you study or learn after listening to the talk? If yes, what will you change, and how and why will you change it? If no, why?

Language Expansion: Educational Choices

A Read the text. Then, complete the definitions with a blue word or phrase.

During their lives, people make many choices about their education. Most young children attend the closest public school, but parents who can pay for private school may choose to send their children to one. If it is a boarding school, the child will live there, too. Some other parents may feel that homeschooling is the best option for their children. Between the ages of 16 and 18, most students start thinking about going to college and getting a degree. They must decide whether to go, where to go, and when to go. These days, taking a gap year is popular because students feel they will have life experiences that will help them in the future. When students enroll at a college, they choose which subject to major in: business and economics are popular majors these days. Students also need to choose whether to live on campus or not. Finally, continuing education is growing more popular because people want to learn useful new skills; so, even adults in their thirties or older may need to make educational choices.

1. _____ education available for adults
2. _____ when parents teach their children at home
3. _____ traveling and working before college
4. _____ a school run by a private company or organization
5. _____ a place where students live and study
6. _____ buildings and land that are part of a school
7. _____ to specialize in a subject at college
8. _____ to start a program of study at a school

Boys from Eton College in the UK taking part in a traditional event

Conversation

B 🎧 55 In pairs, choose words from **A** to complete the conversation. Then, listen and check your answers.

Oscar: Did you ever decide where to send your twins to school, Rachel?

Rachel: We were planning to enroll them in a (1) _____ , but we changed our minds.

Oscar: So are they attending a (2) _____ every day?

Rachel: No. We were going to send them to one, but the fees were too expensive.

Oscar: Yes, private schools can be costly.

Rachel: So my husband said he would (3) _____ them. We tried that for a month, but it was too much work for him.

Oscar: Oh, so where *do* your children go to school?

Rachel: We decided to (4) _____ them in a local public school. Luckily, they love it there!

Oscar: Is that the one just around the corner from your house? If so, that's convenient.

Use **but (we) changed our minds** when you want to introduce a different action.

C Practice the conversation in pairs, taking turns playing each character. Then, create a new conversation about educational choices related to going to college.

Grammar

The Future in the Past	
Use the future in the past to talk about plans for the future that were made in the past (or to refer to plans you made that did not happen).	He **was going to study** German in Berlin, but he had to cancel his plans when his mother got sick.
There are three common patterns for using the future in the past: (1) *was / were going to* + infinitive (2) *was / were* + *-ing* form (3) *would* + infinitive	(1) They **were going to send** their children to a private school. (2) She **was planning** to live on campus. (3) He said he **would major in** economics.

D Read the grammar information. Then, <u>underline</u> the examples of the future in the past in the conversation in **B**. Finally, compare your answers in pairs.

 GOAL CHECK Discuss Educational Choices

Review the educational choices mentioned in **A**. Then, in groups, complete the steps.

1. Discuss which of the choices are made by parents alone, parents and children together, or by the children.

2. Plan a short talk about educational choices in your life. Your talk should mention one educational opportunity you missed, one plan you made that you were not able to do, and one choice you would like to make in the future.

D GOAL Talk about the Value of Play

Reading

A Complete these sentences with your own ideas. Then, share them in groups. Who gave the most interesting answers?

- As a child, my favorite type of play was ...
- The last time I played something was ...
- In my country, people think play is ...

B Read the text. Then, complete each statement with a word or number from the text.

1. Most people think education is serious, but some _____ say it should be fun.

2. Gamification's _____ is not very well known, but the idea is easily understood.

3. One of the advantages of gamification is that students might feel more _____ .

4. An example of gamification in a public space took place roughly _____ years ago.

5. Finland's example shows children can start school at _____ and still do well.

6. Games can help people with PTSD concentrate better and worry less about _____ .

7. Because games have many benefits, they may be good for _____ as well as children.

C In pairs, choose one of the two situations below and come up with an idea to gamify it. Share your idea with the class and explain the benefits.

- Get people to recycle more
- Help people learn a language

✓ GOAL CHECK

In groups, complete these tasks.

1. Discuss how you think you would feel if you could not play for one whole month.

2. Discuss how your life might change if you played for one hour a day for a whole month.

3. Come up with a sentence that explains how important play and games are for humans.

Games:
More Than Just Fun

Many people think they need a good education to get a good job. As a result, they spend hundreds of hours and thousands of dollars a year on their studies. For these people, education is a serious matter. But does it have to be? A growing number of experts say that learning can, and should, be fun.

Gamification is one way to make learning more enjoyable. The name may be unfamiliar, but the idea is easy to understand. One common definition is that gamification is using ideas from games to make non-game situations more fun and enjoyable.

Gamification is becoming popular because studies suggest it has many benefits. For example, students tend to enjoy studying more when their lessons are gamified. Gamification may also help learners concentrate for longer periods and feel more motivation to study. All of these things can build students' confidence and improve their academic results.

Gamification also brings benefits outside of the classroom. A famous example happened in Stockholm, Sweden about ten years ago. The stairs at Odenplan subway station were turned into a piano. When people stepped on them, the stairs made music. Walking up and down the stairs became fun, and the number of people who used the **escalator** went down by about 66 percent.

Gamification is not the only way people can learn while playing. In countries around the world, some schools have a play-based curriculum. The idea is that informal play is better for young children than formal training. The country that is the best example of this is Finland, which has one of the best education systems in the world. Children there do not start formal school until they are seven. Instead of learning to read or do math, younger children spend their time playing creative games.

Doctors are finding that play has benefits for adults, too, and not just in terms of learning. Some people who experience a dangerous situation may develop PTSD (post-traumatic stress disorder). People with PTSD may feel very worried about life. Recent studies show that playing certain video games can help people manage PTSD and improve their lives.

To sum up, games are more than just fun. Famous educators like Maria Montessori have suggested that play is the "work" children should do. Given its many benefits, perhaps adults also should work hard at play.

escalator a moving stair that carries people to higher or lower floors in a building

Students studying in the Student Learning Center at Ryerson University in Toronto, Canada.

Communication

A 🎧 57 Listen to a conversation. Check (✓) the problems that the woman has.

☐ She needs more time for studying.

☐ She forgets details she has learned.

☐ She is finding it hard to concentrate.

☐ She doesn't understand some ideas.

B In pairs, take turns saying which of the problems in **A** you have experienced. Then, discuss any other study problems you have experienced.

C Read the email. Then, in groups, put Tommy's suggestions in order from most to least useful. Finally, share your ideas and reasons with another group.

WORD FOCUS

A **font** is a particular size, weight, and style of letters used in a text.

Hi Mia,

I was thinking about your problem. I have a few suggestions that might help. First, if I were you, I'd visit the Study Center on campus. I'm sure the people who work there could give you some helpful advice. Second, have you heard about this new font called *Sans Forgetica*? Apparently, it can help you remember things better because it makes your brain do more work when reading. Why don't you download the font or at least look up the name to learn more? I've been using it for a month, and I really feel it's helped. Finally, my advice is to take care of your body. I find that my memory and concentration are better when I sleep well, exercise regularly, eat healthily, and drink enough water.

Tommy

D Read the information in the box. Then, reread the email from **C** and answer the questions in pairs.

> **COMMUNICATION SKILL:** Making Recommendations or Suggestions
>
> When you discuss a problem, you may want to recommend or suggest an action or a solution. You can use various expressions to introduce your recommendations and suggestions:
>
> My recommendation is to ... / Why not ... ? / If I were in your shoes, I would ...
>
> In general, it is a good idea to support your suggestions with one or more reasons or benefits. These can be general comments, things you have read or heard, or even personal experiences. You may also wish to mention how somebody can get more information about your suggestion.

1. In the email, which three expressions does Tommy use to introduce his recommendations?

2. How does Tommy support his first suggestion. Does he use a general comment or a personal experience?

3. How does Tommy support both his second and third recommendations?

4. For which suggestion does Tommy explain how to get more information?

Writing

E Choose a common study problem. It can be one of the problems in **A** or another problem, such as having too much work to do or not feeling motivated. Imagine that one of your English-speaking friends is having this problem. Write some suggestions for how he or she could deal with this problem. Use the email in **C** as a model.

F In pairs, share your writing from **E**. Give each other feedback. Then, work together to write improved second drafts.

 GOAL CHECK Describe Problems and Solutions

Complete these steps.

1. Present your ideas from **E** and **F** to the class, using notes rather than reading your writing aloud.

2. In groups, discuss which were the best suggestions you heard, and why.

3. In different groups, discuss some other problems that you or your friends often have and talk about possible solutions to them.

SOLA POWER

Shabana Basij-Rasikh shows teenage girls how to ride a bicycle.

A In pairs, discuss the questions. Use *rarely*, *sometimes*, *usually*, or *always* in your answers.

1. Should governments spend more money on education?

2. Should girls and boys have equal access to education?

3. Do children from poor families have the same access to education as other children?

B In small groups, discuss how governments and individuals can improve education for everyone in a country.

C Watch the first part of the video. Complete this summary with the word or number that the speaker says.

It is important that everyone receive an (1) _____. However, in some places, it may not be available to girls. UNESCO says that around the world, up to (2) _____ million girls are not in school. This is not only a problem for these girls: just one extra (3) _____ of school can help a woman make (4) _____ percent more money when she is an adult. As a result, it can be a problem for (5) _____ when girls are not educated.

D Watch the whole video. Circle the correct option.

1. UNESCO is the United Nations Educational, Scientific and Cultural *Operation* / *Organization*.

2. Shabana Basij-Rasikh's school is called SOLA: the School of *Leadership* / *Learning* Afghanistan.

3. Shabana says that just *six* / *sixteen* percent of women in Afghanistan have a college degree.

4. Shabana mentions that some students at her school learn how to *drive a car* / *ride a bicycle*.

5. Shabana feels that educating a girl will also educate her *family* / *friends* and her community.

6. The common challenge for SOLA students is to *discuss education* / *speak English* all the time.

7. Shabana says her students are the solution to *their family's* / *the world's* most serious issues.

E MY WORLD Are boarding schools popular in your country? Why? Discuss in groups.

155

Look at the photo and answer the questions:

1 What does innovation mean to you?

2 Why is a mobile weather station innovative and useful?

Mark Kamau of BRCK, a company focused on connecting Africa to the internet, holds a prototype for a mobile weather station in Nairobi, Kenya.

UNIT 12 GOALS

A. Speculate about the Future

B. Talk about Positive Outcomes

C. Describe Inventors and Inventions

D. Talk about Good Habits

E. Discuss Purposes and Results

157

GOAL Speculate about the Future

Vocabulary

A Read the text. In groups, discuss whether computers really are the most important invention in history. What other important inventions are there?

Charles Babbage's invention was designed to complete complete complex mathematical problems.

What is the most important invention in history? Some people say it is the computer. This makes sense: we can use them for many purposes, to find solutions to many problems, or to achieve many outcomes.

We think of computers as modern machines. After all, using computers every day is a habit for many of us. However, they have a surprisingly long history. In 1822, a mathematician called Charles Babbage designed a device that could do math. He did not have enough money to build it during his life. However, the Science Museum of London used his plans to build one in the 1980s. The experiment was a success and this early computer worked perfectly.

The invention of microchips in the 1950s was also a significant development. These small parts have led to electronic computers that keep getting smaller, faster, and more powerful. What will happen next? How will people use computers to develop their creativity and improve the world? Nobody knows, but it will be interesting to find out.

B Complete the definitions with the words in blue.

1. _____ : a machine, such as a smartphone, that people use

2. _____ : a positive result or a positive situation

3. _____ : a useful thing, such as the wheel, created by a person

4. _____ : describes a machine that is powered by electricity

5. _____ : describes something very important, special, or large

6. _____ : something good or bad that a person does regularly

7. _____ : the ability to come up with innovative ideas or designs

8. _____ : the reasons for something or the functions of something

9. _____ : the results or effects of a thing that somebody has done

10. _____ : ways to deal with problems or to answer questions

C Expand your vocabulary by learning the verb forms of *creativity*, *invention*, *solution*, and *success*; the adjective forms of *creativity*, *invention*, and *success*; and the noun forms of *electronic* and *significant*. Then learn the noun forms of *creativity* and *invention* that refer to a person.

Grammar

Modals to Discuss the Future

Use *will* + verb to describe things that are certain to happen. If they are not certain, use an adverb like *probably* or *almost certainly*.	Jim **will send** us the solution later today. I **will probably get** a new device soon.
Use *may / might / could* + verb to speculate about things that are possible but not certain to happen.	This innovation **may make** a lot of money. His habits **might change** if we talk to him. The invention **could become** very popular.

 D Complete these sentences in your own words. Then, share your answers in pairs. How similar are your sentences?

1. Next week, I will _____.

2. Next month, I will probably _____.

3. Next year, I may _____.

4. In a few years, I might _____.

5. Within ten years, I could _____.

✓ **GOAL CHECK** Speculate about the Future

In groups, choose *two* inventions from the box and discuss how they might change in the future. When you have finished, share your ideas with the class.

computers
the internet
telephones
televisions
vehicles
watches

Invention	Changes

> I think computers might become smaller.

> I agree. They'll probably become faster, too.

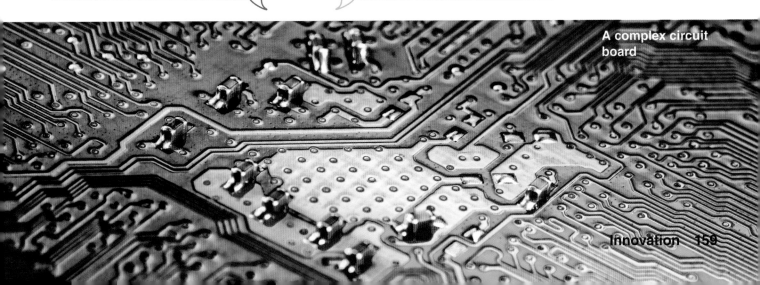

A complex circuit board

GOAL Talk about Positive Outcomes

Listening

A In groups, discuss the questions.

1. How often do you use a computer mouse, a microwave oven, and a tablet computer. When and why do you use it?

2. How would your life change if you could no longer use each device? Be specific.

B 🎧 58 Listen to the beginning of a podcast. What is the speaker mainly going to discuss?

a. Some people who are famous innovators

b. Some ideas for how to be more innovative

c. Some ways competition leads to innovation

C 🎧 59 Listen to the whole podcast and complete the table.

1945	business	Doug Englebart
1960s	the Space Race	Percy Spencer
2010	war	Steve Jobs

Computer mouse	Researched by: (1) _____ Invention date: (2) _____ What competition: (3) _____
Microwave oven	Idea discovered by: (4) _____ Invention date: (5) _____ What struggle: (6) _____
Ipad tablet	Imagined by: (7) _____ Release date: (8) _____ What competition: (9) _____

D There is a saying in English that "Necessity is the mother of invention." This means that when people really need something, they will invent it. In groups, discuss whether the examples mentioned in the podcast support this saying, and why.

PRONUNCIATION: Stress in compound nouns

Compound nouns have two parts. Sometimes the two parts join to make a single word. For these compounds, the stress is usually on the first part.

laptop, notebook

Sometimes the two parts are separate. For these compounds, the stress can be on the first part or the second part. If you are not sure which part to stress, check a dictionary.

laser printer, digital camera

Mars Exploration Rover project staff react as images from the Opportunity rover lander successfully arrived at Mission Control at NASA in Pasadena, California.

 E 🎧 **60** Look at these compound nouns from the talk. <u>Underline</u> where you think the stress will be. Then listen to check your answers.

1. microwave oven
2. Space Race
3. rocket ships
4. computer data
5. smartphones
6. grandmothers

✓ **GOAL CHECK** Talk about Positive Outcomes

In groups, discuss these statements. What do they mean? What examples from your life support each one?

1. Failure often leads to innovation.
2. Great inventions are usually surprisingly simple.
3. Positive thinking leads to positive outcomes.

GOAL Describe Inventors and Inventions

An example of a chindogu invention: a book holder

Language Expansion: Inventors and Inventions

A In pairs, choose the correct phrases (a–h) to complete the definitions of the words in blue.

1. Practical describes people that ___*g*___
2. Curious describes people that _____
3. Smart describes people, ideas, or objects that _____
4. Ambitious describes people that _____
5. Beneficial describes things that _____
6. Enthusiastic describes people that _____
7. Essential describes things that _____
8. Versatile describes people or things that _____

a. are completely necessary or important.

b. are helpful and useful.

c. are interested in knowing how things work.

d. are very excited about something.

e. are very intelligent or clever.

f. can do many things or have many uses.

g. can make or design useful objects.

h. try hard to become rich and successful.

B Write words from **A** in the diagram. Then, in pairs, compare your answers.

Words to describe inventors	Words to describe both	Words to describe inventions

Grammar

Talking about the Future	
To discuss definite plans that you have already made, use either *be going to* + verb, or the present continuous.	(1) _We're going to meet at 9:00 a.m._ (2) _____
To make predictions or to talk about things that are certain to happen, use either *will* + verb or *be going to* + verb.	(3) _____ (4) _____
To describe decisions about the future made at the moment of speaking, use *will* + verb.	(5) _____
To describe scheduled events in the future, use the simple present.	(6) _____

C Complete the grammar chart with the correct example for each description. One example has been done for you.

a. I'm going there tomorrow.

b. We're going to meet at 9:00 a.m.

c. The design museum opens at 10:00.

d. I'm sure Naomi will be OK with the new time.

e. I'll call her later to check.

f. I think it is going to be great.

Conversation

D 🎧 61 In pairs, choose words from **A** to complete the conversation. Then listen and check your answers.

SPEAKING STRATEGY
Use **Sorry?** or **Huh?** to show you don't understand.
Use **OK** to show you do understand.

Abby: There's an exhibition of *chindogu* designs at the design museum. I'm going there tomorrow with Naomi. Do you want to come?

James: Sorry? What kind of designs?

Abby: Chindogu. They're originally from Japan. They're funny inventions such as a book holder!

James: Really? That doesn't sound useful or (1) _____ at all.

Abby: That's the point. Chindogu designs aren't supposed to be (2) _____ or beneficial.

James: Huh? Well, I'm (3) _____ now, so I'd love to come.

Abby: Great! We're going to meet at 9:00 a.m. so we can see the exhibition early.

James: The design museum opens at 10:00, so there's no point in meeting earlier than that.

Abby: OK. Then let's meet at 10:00. I'm sure Naomi will be OK with the new time, but I'll call her later to check.

James: You know, I'd never heard of chindogu before, but I'm really (4) _____ about seeing this exhibition now. I think it's going to be great!

GOAL CHECK Describe Inventors and Inventions

In groups, complete the steps.

1. Come up with an idea for an invention. It could be something practical or a chindogu-style idea.

2. Prepare and practice a talk about your invention. You may want to draw a picture of your idea.

3. Deliver your talk in front of the class. Then discuss which groups came up with the best inventions. Share your decisions and reasons with the rest of the class.

GOAL Talk about Good Habits

Reading

A Read the title of the text. In pairs, discuss what some of these habits might be.

B MY WORLD In groups, discuss if innovation can be learned, or if it is something that some people are naturally good at.

C Read the text. Choose the statement that best summarizes each paragraph. Some are extra.

Paragraph 1 _____   Paragraph 5 _____
Paragraph 2 _____   Paragraph 6 _____
Paragraph 3 _____   Paragraph 7 _____
Paragraph 4 _____

a. A method for remembering innovative ideas

b. A new variation of a traditional expression

c. An answer to a question about innovation

d. Differences between innovation and creativity

e. How new information leads to new ideas

f. Ideas that might be successful in the future

g. Reasons why innovators make high salaries

h. A discussion of why innovation matters

i. The value of doing something every single day

j. The value of questioning traditional ways

D Complete the tasks. Then, in pairs, share your sentences.

1. Write a sentence describing your feelings or thoughts about the text.

2. Write a sentence explaining which of the daily habits you would like to try and why?

✓ GOAL CHECK

In groups, take turns talking about a good habit you have. You should say what the habit is, how often you do it, why it helps you, and how much you recommend it to other people.

Daily Habits of Successful Innovators

1 Some companies act in the way they have always acted. But in our modern world, being innovative is becoming increasingly important. As a result, these companies may find it hard to survive. In contrast, companies like Microsoft, Apple, Google, Amazon, and Tesla find innovative new ways to do things. The huge success of these firms shows the true value of innovation.

2 Innovation is not just important for companies. It has value for individual people, too. Some people feel being innovative is like being tall: you either are, or you aren't. Is this true? Research suggests the opposite: that anybody can become more innovative by having certain habits. This is important, as other studies suggest that innovative people are more likely to have jobs that they enjoy and that pay well.

3 In general, innovative people want to learn. They read often, especially about a wide variety of topics. They talk to people about new ideas. They visit new places. They have new experiences. All of this new information goes into their brains. It can help innovative people see links between ideas that other people cannot see. And this may help them come up with new ideas.

4 Asking questions is another habit that many innovative people have. Innovators want to know how something works, or why something happens, or how long something takes. They also ask questions that help them find better ways to do things. For example, many innovators ask, "Why do we do it this way?" or "Is there a better way to do this?" These questions help them find solutions to problems that other people may not even notice.

5 As a result of learning new things and asking questions, innovative people usually come up with many ideas. In fact, they have so many ideas that they forget some of them. To avoid this problem, innovators often have a way to remember their best ideas. Sometimes they will use a computer or tablet for this purpose. Many innovators, however, prefer old technology: a notebook and a pencil.

6 "If it's not broken, don't fix it" is a common saying. Most people agree with the idea. They think that if something works well, there is no reason to change it. Many innovators feel differently. They constantly look for ways to improve things, even things that are already good. In other words, "Even if it's not broken, make it better" is an innovator's saying.

7 Finally, innovators put in the hours to get better and find new ways to do things. Some of them follow an idea called "Don't break the chain." They set a goal of doing something important every day, such as reading a newspaper article or writing a blog post. After it is done, they mark an X on the calendar for that day. After a while, the calendar has a chain of Xs. Seeing this chain gives them a positive feeling. And in order to keep that positive feeling, they do the action each day.

Writing

> **WRITING SKILL:** Stating Purposes and Results
>
> When you write about something, you may want to say why something happened or why somebody did something. To give this information, you can use *purpose* or *reason* expressions:
>
> • *in order to / so as to / so that / because (of) / due to / as / since*
>
> After you give the purpose or reason, you may want to give the result of what happened. To do this, you can use *result* expressions:
>
> • *so / so ... that / such ... that / as a result (of) / As a result, ...*
>
> Stating the purpose, reason, or result of something will help people follow your ideas.

A Read the information about stating purposes, reasons, and results. Then complete the paragraph with words or phrases from the box. Two answers are possible in some cases.

In the 1930s and 1940s in Finland, many babies died soon after they were born. (1) _____ improve this situation, the government gave new mothers a box. The box had clothes to keep the baby warm as well as other useful things. And (2) _____ the box also had a mattress and blankets, it could be used as the baby's bed. (3) _____ of the boxes, fewer babies died. The effect was (4) _____ positive (5) _____ the government of Finland has continued to give baby boxes away. In addition, other countries have recently begun to copy this innovative idea.

Finnish baby box with sleeping baby

B In groups, rewrite the paragraph in **A** by following these steps.

1. Rewrite the first sentence so that it starts with "Many babies died ..."
2. Rewrite the second sentence so that it starts with "The government gave ..."
3. Rewrite the third sentence so that it includes the phrase "such as" in the middle.
4. Rewrite the fourth sentence so that it starts with "The box could be used as ..."
5. Rewrite the fifth sentence so that it starts with "Due to ..."
6. Rewrite the sixth sentence so that it uses the expression "such ... that ..."
7. Rewrite the final sentence so that it ends with "... as well."

C In pairs, write a paragraph based on these notes. Use the paragraph in **A** as a model.

- some babies who are born early die → cannot stay warm
- some students who attended Stanford Univ → innovative solution
- created a special blanket → Embrace Care infant warmer
- blanket can be heated → electricity / hot water
- stays warm for hours → safer for babies
- Embrace products helped 1,000,000 early babies → cheap / easy-to-use

Communication

D In groups, discuss these questions. Give reasons for your opinions.

1. Which is more innovative: Finland's baby boxes or Embrace Care infant warmers?
2. What emotions would new parents who get the baby box or the Embrace Care blanket feel?
3. What other solutions to its problem could Finland have adopted?
4. What other solutions to keeping babies warm can you come up with?

E In pairs, read the situation and discuss a solution. Then present your solution to the class. Use expressions of purpose, reason, and result.

> In most countries in the world, women spend much more time looking after young babies than men do. This is not fair. In order to improve the situation, your government wants to get men to spend more time looking after infants.

 GOAL CHECK Discuss Purposes and Results

Complete the steps.

1. Write three things you have done this week. Make a note of your purpose and the result of what you did.
2. In groups, take turns sharing the things you did, your purpose for doing them, and the results of what you did.

TEDTALKS

WHY YOU SHOULD MAKE USELESS THINGS

SIMONE GIERTZ

Inventor, Robotics Enthusiast

Simone's **idea worth spreading** is that sometimes useful innovation can come from "useless" play or just from asking questions.

A In a group, discuss what Simone Giertz's **idea worth spreading** means and how true you think it is.

B Watch the first part of the talk. In groups, discuss which of Simone's inventions is your favorite. Why?

C Predict how to complete each quotation from the talk with a word from the box. Some words are extra. Then watch the second part of the talk to check your answers.

boring / fun	smart / stupid
difficult / easy	useful / useless
false / true	

1. "But building things with hardware, especially if you're teaching yourself, is something that's really _____ to do."

2. "And even though I didn't realize it at the time, building _____ things was actually quite _____."

3. "And identifying a problem is the first step in my process of building a _____ machine."

4. "Building useless machines is really _____, but how is this in any way or form a business?"

5. "I often get asked if I think I'm ever going to build something _____, and maybe someday I will."

6. "To me that's the _____ beauty of making useless things, because it's this acknowledgment that you don't always know what the best answer is."

D Work in a group. Complete these tasks.

1. Summarize Simone's reasons for creating her inventions. Then discuss how good you think these reasons are. Why?

2. In Lesson **C** you learned about *chindogu* inventions. Discuss how similar Simone's inventions are to chindogu.

3. In Lesson **D** you learned about some habits of innovative people. Discuss which of these habits you think Simone probably has, and why.

4. Think of a problem and discuss what invention (useful or useless) Simone might develop to solve it. Then share your problem and invention with the class.

E **MY WORLD** Work in a different group. Take turns talking about a time when you did something playful or "useless" that led to real innovation.

Simone Giertz tries out her invention.

169

Grammar Reference

UNIT 1

Lesson A

Present Perfect Tenses

The present perfect (*has / have* + past participle) and continuous (*has / have* + *been* + present participle) both refer to past situations connected to the present.	I **have lived** here for a long time. I**'ve been living** here for a long time.
Form the present perfect as follows: subject + *has / 's / have / 've* (+ *not*) + past participle (+ object) Form questions as follows: *Has (n't) / Have (n't)* + subject + past participle (+ object) + ?	He**'s lived** there. He **hasn't lived** there. **Has** he **lived** there? **Hasn't** he **lived** there?
Form the present perfect continuous as follows: subject + *has / 's / have / 've* + (*not*) *been* + present participle (+ object) Form questions as follows: *Has (n't) / Have (n't)* + subject + *been* + present participle (+ object) + ?	He**'s been living** there. He **hasn't been living** there. **Has** he **been living** there? **Hasn't** he **been living** there?
In most cases, use the present perfect: 1. to emphasize that an event has been completed. 2. with verbs that take no time to complete. 3. to emphasize that an action will not be repeated. 4. for things that have been true for a very long time. 5. with stative verbs connected to our minds or senses.	1. He **has told** us already. 2. She**'s** just **started** a new job. 3. You**'ve given** us some great news! 4. People **have lived** in this city for thousands of years. 5. You**'ve known** me since I was a kid.
In most cases, use the present perfect continuous: 1. to emphasize how long something continued. 2. to describe past actions that are still continuing.	1. They**'ve been waiting** for hours. 2. It **has been raining** since yesterday.

Some time expressions are common with both tenses: 1. Use *for* to say how long something has continued. 2. Use *since* to indicate when something started. 3. Use *during / for / in the last* + period to say how long or how often. 4. Use *recently* or *lately* to discuss recent events or actions. 5. Use *ever* or *never* to talk or ask about things you have done or not done in your life.	1. We**'ve worked** together **for** years. 2. We**'ve been working** together **since** we finished college. 3. I**'ve been** there three times **in the last 10 years**. 4. She**'s been calling** me a lot **recently**. 5. I**'ve never** visited Japan or Korea.

A Complete each sentence with a time expression from the box.

during the summer	for three days	in the last year
never	recently	since 9 o'clock

1. We've been staying at this hotel _____.
2. They've been waiting _____ this morning.
3. _____, Jude has moved to a new house four times.
4. Issie has made several new friends _____.
5. Surprisingly, he has _____ learned to swim.
6. _____, I've gone swimming almost every day.

B Answer the questions with complete sentences. Use either the present perfect or the present perfect continuous.

1. How long have you been living in your current home?
2. How many times have you checked your phone today?
3. What is your favorite movie and how many times have you seen it?
4. Who is your best friend and how often do you see him or her?
5. Who is your favorite singer and how long have you liked him or her?
6. What is something you are waiting for and how long have you been waiting for it?

Lesson C

So … That	
Use *so* … (*that*) + a clause to explain and give the result of something. The word(s) after *so* give the reason, and the clause after *that* gives the result. (Note: *that* is optional.) Several *so … that* patterns are possible: 1. *so* + adjective phrase (+ *that*) + clause 2. *so* + adverb phrase (+ *that*) + clause 3. *so* + *many* / *few* + countable noun phrase (+ *that*) + clause 4. *so* + *much* / *little* + uncountable noun phrase (+ *that*) + clause	1. The movie is **so good that** I've seen it three times. 2. She left **so quickly that** we couldn't say goodbye. 3. There are **so many good jobs in this city that** thousands of people have moved here. 4. I have **so little money this month that** I cannot even take the bus to work.

A Rewrite each sentence pair into one sentence using *so … that*.

1. He uses his phone often. The battery runs out very quickly. _____

2. She has lots of money. She can buy whatever she wants. _____

3. The cake was delicious. I ate all of it. Now I don't feel well! _____

4. The store had few customers. It had to close down. _____

5. Matt's idea was good. Everyone agreed with it immediately. _____

6. Jo answered the questions quickly. She was the first to finish. _____

UNIT 2

Lesson A

Infinitives and *-ing* Forms 1	
A few verbs can take either infinitives or *-ing* forms, but with a major difference in meaning.	He **stopped to buy** chocolate. (i.e., The reason he stopped was to buy chocolate.)
For example, *forget*, *remember*, *stop*, and *try*.	He **stopped buying** chocolate. (i.e., He no longer buys chocolate.)
To say that an action didn't happen, use the correct form of *does* + *not* before the main verb.	They <u>didn't</u> **promise to call** him. (i.e., They didn't make any promise about calling.) She <u>doesn't</u> **like taking** the bus each day. (i.e., She has to take the bus, but she dislikes it.)
It is also possible to make a negative sentence by putting the word *not* between *to* and the base verb (for infinitives) or before the *-ing* form.	They **promised** <u>not</u> **to call** him. (i.e., They promised that they would not call.) She **likes** <u>not</u> **taking** the bus each day. (i.e., She is happy that she doesn't take the bus.)
For questions, use regular question word order.	Did he **manage to finish** all his work? Why do you **hate using** the telephone?

A Circle the correct form (infinitive or *-ing*) to complete each sentence.

1. He forgot *to buy* / *buying* orange juice, so he has to go back to the store.

2. We stopped *to shop* / *shopping* at that store because of its high prices.

3. I promised *to finish* / *finishing* all of the work on time, but I couldn't do it.

4. She remembered *to visit* / *visiting* the same place when she was a child.

B Rewrite each sentence as a negative sentence and then again as a question.

1. The children enjoyed listening to their teacher tell them a story.

   _____

   _____

2. The friends agreed to meet in the cafe on the corner of Main Street.

   _____

   _____

3. Andrew discussed looking for a new job with his friend Martina.

   _____

   _____

4. I hated studying mathematics and science when I was a child.

_____

_____

Lesson C

Could, May, and Might

For negative sentences with *may*, or *might*, add **not** after the modal and before the base verb. (Note that it is uncommon to use *not* after *could* to express uncertainty or possibility. Also, note that it is uncommon to use the contracted form (*n't*) after *may* or *might*.)	It **may** / **might not arrive** tomorrow.
For questions with *could*, *may*, or *might*, it is most common to use a phrase like *Do you think* to begin the sentence and then normal word order.	**Do you think** he **might** be sick?
In formal language, sometimes the modal is the question word and question word order is used.	**Could** he be sick?

A Rewrite each sentence as a negative statement and then again as a question.

1. They might visit our house next week.

_____

_____

2. He may be available to help us later.

_____

_____

3. I may have lost my textbook and laptop.

_____

_____

4. The halo effect might have influenced us.

_____

_____

UNIT 3

Lesson A

The Passive 1

Form the passive with *be* + the past participle of the main verb.	Unfortunately, trees **are removed** to make room for farming.
Use the passive with any verb tense.	Thousands of acres of forest **have been destroyed** in recent years.

Use the passive: 1. when the agent (the doer) is not known or not important. 2. to emphasize the object of the verb.	1. Oil **can be refined** into gasoline and diesel fuel for cars, trucks, and ships. 2. Six countries in the region **were affected** by drought last year.
Use a *by* phrase to say who or what does something (the agent).	New trees **are being planted by local children**.

A Rewrite the sentences in your notebook in the passive. Use a *by* phrase when needed.

1. People use coal and oil for heating and transportation.
2. Conservation groups raise money for environmental projects.
3. Extreme weather has caused many problems in recent years.
4. Immigrants brought invasive species to Australia during the 1800s.
5. Palm oil plantations are causing deforestation in Southeast Asia.
6. In many parts of the world, people are conserving energy.
7. One company developed an excellent land management plan.
8. Recycling has kept tons of paper and plastic out of landfills.

B Complete the sentences with an appropriate agent.

1. Those nests in that tree were made by _____.

2. This textbook was published by _____.

3. Oil is being used as fuel by _____.

4. My favorite kind of shampoo is made by _____.

5. Rising sea levels are caused by _____.

Lesson C

The Past Perfect

Use the past perfect to talk about something that happened before another event in the past: subject + *had* + (*not*) + past participle	The game warden arrived on Wednesday and saw that many fish **had died**. They **had not had** problems in that lake previously.

The simple past is often used with words such as *before* or *after* that make the time relationship clear. Both forms are grammatically correct.	Cats **had come** to the island on ships **before** the rabbits arrived. Cats **came** to the island on ships **before** the rabbits **arrived**.

A Read each sentence and underline what happens first.

1. The Nile Perch had been a river fish before it was brought to Lake Victoria.
2. The lake had not had such a large predator before the perch arrived.
3. By the late 1980s, the perch population had grown enormously.
4. James called his mother after he finished playing soccer.
5. Before the sun went down, Rita found a good place to watch the fireworks.

UNIT 4

Lesson A

Infinitives and *-ing* Forms 2	
Use a gerund or an infinitive as the subject of a sentence.	**Helping** people is rewarding. **To help** people is rewarding.
Use an infinitive to give more information about a noun or adjective.	I'm **determined to get** a good job.
-ing forms can be the object of a preposition.	You can achieve your goals **by working** hard.
Verb + infinitive Use infinitives after certain verbs, including: agree decide hope learn need promise want	I **try to find** new opportunities every day.
Verb + gerund Use gerunds after certain verbs, including: avoid consider enjoy finish give up stop	They **avoid doing** work after the work day finishes.
Verb + infinitive or gerund Use infinitives or gerunds after certain verbs, including: begin continue hate like love prefer	I **prefer to pay** in cash. I **prefer paying** in cash.

A Unscramble the words to make statements.

1. nap / good / taking / for / a / in / afternoon / is / the / you

   _____
   _____

2. marathons / are / they / good / running / at

   _____
   _____

3. enough / for / the / needs / she / time / study / to / exam

   _____
   _____

4. many / staying / late / up / common / is / a / habit / people / of

   _____
   _____

5. hobby / is / jogging / her / favorite

   _____
   _____

B Complete the sentences with the correct form of the words in parentheses.

1. I've had _____ (trouble / stay) up late.
2. _____ (have / friends) is good because it helps you feel less lonely.
3. Are you _____ (have / difficulty) falling asleep?
4. I'm wasting _____ (time / look) for the store.
5. It would be _____ (fun / learn) from you.

Lesson C

The Passive 2	
Form the negative passive by placing *not* after *be* or after the modal.	The money **is not** usually **deposited**. The receipt **will not be printed** automatically.
Notice the word order of questions in the passive.	**Are** credit cards **accepted** here? **Where was** the package **delivered**?

A Underline the passive in the sentences. Then rewrite the sentences in the negative.

1. The instructions were followed by the team.

   _____

2. We are affected by changes in our work places.

   _____

3. My office space has been reduced.

_____

4. Action is being taken to protect our benefits.

_____

5. We are being given less vacation time this year.

_____

B Rewrite the sentences as questions.

1. Officials have reported that productivity is better.

_____

2. The office is changing our work schedule.

_____

3. All of us are affected by the changes.

_____

4. She has been given a raise.

_____

5. She is being given a promotion.

_____

UNIT 5

Lesson A

Unreal Conditionals	
Unreal conditionals that refer to unlikely events are often called _second conditionals_.	_if_ + subject + simple past, subject + would + base form of verb If I **was** sick, I **wouldn't go** to class.
Unreal conditionals that refer to impossible events are often called _third conditionals_.	_If_ + subject + past perfect, subject + _would_ + _have_ + past participle If I **hadn't gotten** sick, I **would have come** to class.
For both second and third conditionals, using different modals can change the meaning.	If he had a phone, he **would** / **might** / **could** call you.
In questions, use question word order in the result part of the sentence, not in the conditional part.	**Would** he **have helped** if I had told him? ~~He would have helped if had I told him?~~
In negative sentences, put _not_ in the condition clause or the result clause, depending on the situation. If _not_ is in both clauses, the two negatives result in a positive meaning.	If I had left, I **would _not_ have been** sad. (I did not leave, so now I am sad.) If I **had _not_ left**, I **would have been** sad. (I did leave, so now I am happy.) If I **had_n't_ left**, I **would_n't_ have been** sad. (I did leave, so now I am sad.)

A Rewrite second conditional sentences as third conditionals and third conditionals as second conditionals. Follow the example.

Example   If he had finished early, he would have won. →
            If he finished early, he would win.

1. Would you answer if I called you?

_____
_____

2. If you won some money, what would you buy?

_____
_____

3. If they had lost it, I might have found it.

_____
_____

4. I could have visited if I had had more time.

_____
_____

5. If I sent the message, he wouldn't like it.

_____
_____

B Use a word from the box to complete each sentence. In some cases, several answers are possible.

could	if	might	not	would

1. Dinosaurs might have survived if a comet had _____ hit Earth a long time ago.

2. If climate change continued, how _____ the weather in your country change?

3. If the hurricane had struck the city, some people _____ definitely have died.

4. Humans _____ survive a future disaster if we lived on both Mars and Earth.

5. Protect your head _____ an earthquake happens when you are in a building.

Lesson C

Using _Wish_ and _Hope_
In sentences with _wish_ or _hope_, the word _that_ is not necessary. However, it is a good idea to include it for two reasons. First, it may help listeners or readers follow your ideas. Second, using _that_ reminds you that you need a new clause (with subject and verb).

To say what you want to do in a formal way, use *wish to* + verb. Don't use *wish* (+ *that*) + simple past.	He **wishes to leave**. ~~He wishes that he left.~~
To talk about plans, use *hope to* + verb as well as *hope* (+ *that*) + simple present.	I **hope to get** a new job. I **hope that I get** a new job.
To say that you hope somebody was not affected by a bad situation, use *hope* (+ *that*) + subject + simple past.	I **hope that** your house **wasn't damaged** by the storm.

A Complete each sentence with *hope* or *wish*. In some cases, both may be correct.

1. I asked them about their plans and they said they _____ to become doctors.

2. We all really _____ that you weren't affected by the hurricane last month.

3. They definitely _____ that the flood hadn't damaged their home so badly.

4. I _____ that this city does not experience any more natural disasters this year.

B Write some sentences about your own hopes and wishes.

1. _____
_____

2. _____
_____

3. _____
_____

4. _____
_____

UNIT 6

Lesson A

Reported Speech

In indirect speech, the tense of the original verb usually shifts back in time. For example:
- (present) *do* or *doing* → (past) *did* or *was doing*
- (present perfect) *have done* or *have been doing* → (past perfect) *had done* or *had been doing*
- (past) *did* or *was doing* → (past perfect) *had done* or *had been doing*
- (modals) *will do* / *can do* / *shall do* → ("past" modals) *would do* / *could do* / *should do*

However, there is no change in these cases:
- when the original verb is in the past perfect
- or for "past" modals like *could, would, should, might*
- if the original statement is still true or has not happened yet.

Reported questions use normal word order and do not end with a question mark. To report *wh-* questions, use the *wh-* word to introduce the reported speech. To report *yes* / *no* questions, use *if* or *whether* to introduce the reported speech.	She asked, "When did you do it?" → She asked <u>when</u> I had done it.
	She asked, "Can you do it?" → She asked <u>if</u> they could do it.

A Rewrite the direct speech sentences into indirect speech using the verbs in parentheses. Remember to change the verb and pronoun if necessary.

Example   Mark said, "I did it quickly." (explained) → Mark explained that he had done it quickly.

1. They said, "We will do it soon." _____
_____ (said).

2. Jane said, "I have been doing it."_____
_____ (mentioned).

3. I said to him, "You should do it." _____
_____ (told).

4. Pete said, "I haven't done it yet." _____
_____ (explained).

5. Everyone said, "We can do it." _____
_____ (shouted).

B Rewrite the sentences as indirect speech questions.

Example   Ann said, "Have you seen the display?" → Ann asked if I had seen the display.

1. Bob asked, "Where is your painting?"
_____
_____

2. Carl asked, "Who took the photograph?"
_____
_____

3. Deb asked, "Did the painting sell?"
_____
_____

4. Ed asked, "Is this artist a genius?"
_____
_____

5. Farah asked, "When was it painted?"
_____
_____

Lesson C

Adjective Clauses 1

If the adjective clause gives information about something that belongs to a person, use *whose* instead of *who* or *that*.	The woman **whose art is on display in the gallery** is my friend. The man over there, **whose name I have forgotten**, is an artist.

A Underline the adjective clauses in sentences 1 to 3. Then complete sentences 4 to 6 with *who, whose, which,* or *that*.

1. A potter, who makes pots or other kinds of dishes, is one kind of ceramic artist.

2. The name for a person who takes photographs as their job is a photographer.

3. Botticelli and Caravaggio, who were both born in Italy, are world-famous painters.

4. Michelangelo, _____ was also from Italy, was a great painter and sculptor _____ most famous work is probably the ceiling of the Sistine Chapel.

5. American architect Louis Sullivan, _____ died in 1924, is famous for the expression "form follows function," _____ had a big impact on other architects.

6. Joseph Michael is a media artist _____ makes art _____ mixes photography and video.

UNIT 7

Lesson A

The Passive 3

Use passive modals with the present perfect to: 1. talk about something that we are unsure about. 2. describe something that did not happen.	1. The tickets **may have been sent**. (I don't know if the tickets were sent or not.) 2. The tickets **should have been sent** yesterday. (The tickets were not sent.)

A Complete these sentences with a passive verb from the box.

can be used	has been closed	have been sold
were lost	will be finished	

1. Because of the accident, the road _____ .

2. The repairs to your car _____ on time.

3. All of our suitcases _____ by the airline.

4. Drones _____ to deliver packages or pizza.

5. The antique bicycles _____ to a new buyer.

B Rewrite these active sentences as passive sentences.

Example He might have done it. → It might have been done (by him).

1. She must have seen it. _____ _____

2. They could have lost it. _____ _____

3. You can easily drive it. _____ _____

4. We may have taken it. _____ _____

5. He might cancel it. _____ _____

Lesson C

Indirect Questions

Some question phrases can introduce indirect questions. With these phrases, the sentence should end with a question mark. • Could I ask … ? • Would you mind explaining … ? • Do you remember … ? • Do you have any idea … ?	**Could I ask** where you went on vacation? **Would you mind explaining** why you did it? **Do you remember** when we last took a trip? **Do you have any idea** what the man said?
Some statement phrases can also introduce indirect questions. With these phrases, the sentence should end with a period. • I want to know … • I need to find out … • I don't know … • I'd like to ask …	**I want to know** where you went on vacation. **I need to find out** why you did it. **I don't know** when we last took a trip. **I'd like to ask** what the man said.

A Unscramble the phrases to make indirect questions.

Example   where / I want / you're going / to know →
I want to know where you're going.

1. remember / of your / do you / first teacher / the name _____
_____

2. when you / where and / I'd like / were born / to ask
_____
_____

3. do you / the bicycle / have any / invented / idea who _____
_____

4. ask how / could I / often you / vacation / take a
_____
_____

5. why you / to know / chose to / I want / study English _____
_____

UNIT 8

Lesson A

Tag Questions

If the sentence has an auxiliary or modal verb, use the same auxiliary or modal in the tag.	She**'s** nice. → She's nice, **isn't** she? He **can't** do it. → He can't do it, **can** he?
In other cases, use the correct tense and negative form of *do* in the tag.	We liked it. → We liked it, **didn't** we?
Match the noun or pronoun in the sentence with a pronoun in the tag question.	The book is new. **The book** is new, isn't **it**?
In spoken English, you can use *right* as the tag word. These questions do not have a pronoun.	It's expensive. → It's expensive, **right**? They did it. → They did it, **right**?

A Complete these sentences with the correct tag and pronoun. Remember to use a positive tag for negative sentences and a negative tag for positive ones.

1. Susan used to go running every day, _____ ?

2. That gym isn't a good place to work out, _____ ?

3. John and Pete can play baseball well, _____ ?

4. Mountain bikes cost a lot of money, _____ ?

5. The team didn't win any of its games last season, _____ ?

6. You and I should play a board game, _____ ?

B Write six new sentences that use the same tags and pronouns as in the sentences in A.

1. _____
2. _____
3. _____
4. _____
5. _____

Lesson C

Adjective Clauses 2

If an adjective clause gives information about a thing that belongs to somebody or something, use *whose* instead of *who*, *which*, or *that*.	A: Who won the race? The athlete **that** is wearing the red shirt? B: No, the one **whose** shirt is blue.

A Complete these sentences with *who, whose, which,* or *that*. In some cases, two answers are possible.

1. Alexandra scored the goal _____ won the championship.

2. The team has many athletes _____ come from South America.

3. The sporting event has tickets _____ cost between $40 and $100.

4. The coach _____ team lost 10 games in a row has just been fired.

5. She is a very professional player _____ could help any team win.

6. He has an injury to his muscle, _____ will stop him from playing today.

B Rewrite the sentences in A by changing just three words. Then share the changes you made in pairs.

1. _____
_____

2. _____
_____

3. _____
_____

4. _____
_____

5. _____
_____

6. _____
_____

UNIT 9

Lesson A

Negative Questions

Sometimes we can use negative questions to offer something in a polite way.	**Wouldn't** you **like** something to eat? **Can't** I **get** you anything to drink?
To avoid confusion, give a long answer for a negative question, rather than just saying "Yes" or "No."	A: **Isn't** she **allergic** to nuts? B: Yes. B: Yes, she is (allergic to them). C: No. C: No, she isn't (allergic to nuts).

A Choose the best negative question from the box to respond to each question or statement.

> Can't I get you a drink?   Doesn't he like reading?
> Don't you think it's funny?   Hasn't he finished it yet?
> Shouldn't you wait for a sale?

1. **A:** I'm going to buy a phone today.
   B: _____
2. **A:** Michael just wants to watch TV.
   B: _____
3. **A:** Sam is still doing that project.
   B: _____
4. **A:** The weather is really hot today.
   B: _____
5. **A:** Wow! This movie is so boring.
   B: _____

B Rewrite the statements, *yes / no* questions, and tag questions as negative questions.

1. You should wear a helmet when you go biking.
   _____

2. Using a knife that isn't sharp is dangerous, isn't it?
   _____

3. You are surprised that allergies can be dangerous.
   _____

4. Do you enjoy doing risky activities like climbing?
   _____

5. You have lived in large cities all of your life.
   _____

Lesson C

Adverbials of Time

The time expressions in time adverbials are often conjunctions like *after*, *as*, *before*, *since*, *until*, *when*, or *while*. In most cases, conjunctions are followed by a subject and verb.	It happened **after the meeting took place**. She has worked here **since she was twenty**. We will stay **until you have finished it**. I was happy **when I was living in that city**.
1. Sometimes, the time adverbial can be reduced after a conjunction. 2. In reduced adverbials, the subject is dropped and the verb is turned into an *-ing* form.	1. They talked about it **before they met him**. → They talked about it **before meeting** him. 2. We left the office **after we finished the work**. → We left the office **after finishing the work**.
The time expressions in time adverbials can also be prepositions like *after*, *before*, *during*, *since*, or *until*. Use a noun or noun phrase, not a subject and verb, after a preposition.	It happened **after the meeting**. She has worked here **since 2011**. We will stay **until the end of the work day**. I was happy **during my time in that city**.

A Complete these questions with a clause or phrase from the box.

> after exercising or playing sports
> before you came to this school
> if you have some good news
> since the year of your birth
> when you were 10 years old

1. Where were you studying _____
   _____ ?
2. What was your best friend's name _____
   _____ ?
3. What do you like to do _____
   _____ ?
4. Who will you tell first _____
   _____ ?
5. Who is somebody you have known _____
   _____ ?

UNIT 10

Lesson A

Modals to Discuss the Past

To talk about something that definitely (or almost definitely) did not happen in the past, use *can't / cannot* + *have* + past participle.	This statue looks old, but it **can't have come from** ancient Rome because it was made just 20 years ago.
Modals that can be used to talk about what *must*, *might*, or *can't have* happened are called modals of deduction.	

A Complete each sentence with *can't*, *might*, or *must*.

1. Jon _____ have bought a new car because he doesn't have any money right now.

2. I can't find my phone. I _____ have left it on the train or perhaps I left it at home.

3. She _____ have called earlier, but I haven't checked my messages, so I'm not sure.

4. Joe _____ have been really disappointed when he learned that he had lost his job.

5. Su doesn't have a passport, so she _____ have taken a vacation in another country.

B Replace the modal in each sentence in **A** with the modals in parentheses. Change the rest of the sentence, too, so that it makes sense.

1. (could) _____
_____

2. (must) _____
_____

3. (can't) _____
_____

4. (may) _____
_____

5. (must) _____
_____

Lesson C

Noun Clauses

Noun clauses do not express a complete idea, so they cannot act as a complete sentence.	*What he should do.* He did not know **what he should do**.
The following words often begin noun clauses: *how, that, what(ever), when(ever), where(ver), whether, which(ever), who(m)(ever), why*	We can go there on **whichever day you want**. **Whether his plan will work or not** is a mystery. Her strength is **that she always works hard**.

A Complete these sentences in your own words.

1. _____ where they should go.

2. _____ how much it will cost.

3. Why she told him _____.

4. Whatever you want to do _____.

5. _____ with what he said about it.

UNIT 11

Lesson A

Could have, Should have, and Would have

The modals *could have*, *should have*, and *would have* are sometimes called modals of lost opportunity because we use them to imagine or discuss something that did not happen.	They **could have** gone to the movies, but didn't. She **should have** saved her money. I **would have** eaten the cake, but it was old.

A Complete each sentence with *could have*, *should have*, or *would have*. In some cases, two answers are possible.

1. You _____ told me that you were coming. I would have picked you up at the airport.

2. I _____ bought a cheaper computer, but this one will help me do my work more quickly.

3. It _____ been a good idea to go on vacation last month. The weather was better then.

4. I'm not surprised that your teacher was disappointed: you _____ done your homework!

5. If I had practiced more, I think I _____ become a professional basketball player.

B Rewrite each sentence in **A** using the negative form of the modal: *couldn't have*, *shouldn't have*, or *wouldn't have*. Change the rest of the sentence, too, so that it makes sense.

1. _____
_____

2. _____
_____

3. _____
_____

4. _____
_____

5. _____
_____

Lesson C

The Future in the Past

To express a future in the past idea, use the past tense of verbs like *want*, *plan*, or *hope* + *to* + infinitive.	When I was a child, I **wanted** to be a teacher. Last year, I **planned** to major in biology, but I changed my mind. We **hoped** to move into a larger house.

A Rewrite these sentences using the future in the past.

1. The school is going to buy some new technology for the classrooms.

   _____

   _____

2. The teachers want the children in first grade to spend more time playing.

   _____

   _____

3. The students are planning to do their homework over the weekend.

   _____

   _____

4. The boarding school is going to reduce its prices starting next year.

   _____

   _____

5. According to an expert, online degrees are going to be very popular.

   _____

   _____

UNIT 12

Lesson A

Future Modals

To talk about future ability, use *will / may / might (not) be able to* + verb.	I **will be able to send** you the money later. They **may not be able to finish** on time.
To talk about things that will be necessary in the future, use *will / may / might (not) have to* + verb.	We**'ll have to leave** very soon, I'm afraid. I **might not have to go** to Brazil on Friday.
Note that it is common to include a time marker such as *later* or *next week* in sentences that refer to the future.	

A Complete these sentences in your own words.

1. In the future, I will _____. How about you?

2. Next year, I might _____. What do you think about that?

3. I think computers will soon be able to _____. Do you agree?

4. Next week, I might have to _____. What about you?

5. Somebody might invent a device to _____. Would you buy it?

B Answer the questions in **A**.

1. _____

2. _____

3. _____

4. _____

5. _____

Lesson C

Talking about the Future

Use *will* or *be going to* + verb to talk about the future.	Space exploration **will be** even more international in the future. Space exploration **is going to be** even more international in the future.
Use the present continuous to talk about definite future events.	We **are flying** to Mexico City next month.
Use the simple present to talk about scheduled events in the future.	Our train **leaves** at 8:30 a.m.

A Make predictions about what the things in the box will be like in the future.

> communication   the environment   food   transportation

1. _____

2. _____

3. _____

4. _____

Spelling Rules for Verbs Ending in -s and -es

1. Add -s to most verbs.	like-like**s** sit-sit**s**
2. Add -es to verbs that end in -ch, -s, -sh, -x, or -z.	catch-catch**es** miss-miss**es** wash-wash**es** mix-mix**es** buzz-buzz**es**
3. Change the -y to -i and add -es when the base form ends in a consonant + -y.	cry-cr**ies** carry-carr**ies**
4. Do not change the -y when the base form ends in a vowel + -y.	pay-pay**s** stay-stay**s**
5. Some verbs are irregular in the third-person singular -s form of the simple present.	be-**is** go-**goes** do-**does** have-**has**

Spelling Rules for Verbs Ending in -ing

1. Add -ing to the base form of most verbs.	eat-eat**ing** do-do**ing** speak-speak**ing** carry-carry**ing**
2. When the verb ends in a consonant + -e, drop the -e and add -ing.	ride-rid**ing** write-writ**ing**
3. For one-syllable verbs that end in a consonant + a vowel + a consonant (CVC), double the final consonant and add -ing. Do not double the final consonant for verbs that end in CVC when the final consonant is -w, -x, or -y.	stop-stop**ping** sit-sit**ting** show-show**ing** fix-fix**ing** stay-stay**ing**
4. For two-syllable verbs that end in CVC and have stress on the first syllable, add -ing. Do not double the final consonant. For two-syllable verbs that end in CVC and have stress on the last syllable, double the final consonant and add -ing.	ENter-enter**ing** LISTen-listen**ing** beGIN-beginn**ing** ocCUR-occurr**ing**

Spelling Rules for Verbs Ending in -ed

1. Add -ed to the base form of most verbs that end in a consonant.	start-start**ed** talk-talk**ed**
2. Add -d if the base form of the verb ends in -e.	dance-danc**ed** live-liv**ed**
3. When the base form of the verb ends in a consonant + -y, change the -y to -i and add -ed. Do not change the -y to -i when the verb ends in a vowel + -y.	cry-cr**ied** worry-worr**ied** stay-stay**ed**
4. For one-syllable verbs that end in a consonant + a vowel + a consonant (CVC), double the final consonant and add -ed. Do not double the final consonant of verbs that end in -w, -x, or -y.	stop-stop**ped** rob-rob**bed** follow-follow**ed** fix-fix**ed** play-play**ed**
5. For two-syllable verbs that end in CVC and have stress on the first syllable, add -ed. Do not double the final consonant. For two-syllable verbs that end in CVC and have stress on the last syllable, double the final consonant and add -ed.	ORder-order**ed** HAPpen-happen**ed** ocCUR-occur**red** preFER-prefer**red**

Spelling Rules for Comparative and Superlative Forms

	Adjective/ Adverb	Comparative	Superlative
1. Add -er or -est to one-syllable adjectives and adverbs.	tall fast	tall**er** fast**er**	tall**est** fast**est**
2. Add -r or -st to adjectives that end in -e.	nice	nice**r**	nice**st**
3. Change the -y to -i and add -er or -est to two-syllable adjectives and adverbs that end in -y.	easy happy	eas**ier** happ**ier**	eas**iest** the happ**iest**
4. Double the final consonant and add -er or -est to one-syllable adjectives or adverbs that end in a consonant + a vowel + a consonant (CVC).	big hot	big**ger** hot**ter**	big**gest** hot**test**

Common Irregular Verbs

Base Form	Simple Past	Past Participle	Base Form	Simple Past	Past Participle
begin	began	begun	make	made	made
break	broke	broken	meet	met	met
bring	brought	brought	pay	paid	paid
buy	bought	bought	put	put	put
come	came	come	read	read	read
do	did	done	ride	rode	ridden
drink	drank	drunk	run	ran	run
drive	drove	driven	say	said	said
eat	ate	eaten	see	saw	seen
feel	felt	felt	send	sent	sent
get	got	gotten	sit	sat	sat
give	gave	given	sleep	slept	slept
go	went	gone	speak	spoke	spoken
have	had	had	swim	swam	swum
hear	heard	heard	take	took	taken
hurt	hurt	hurt	tell	told	told
know	knew	known	think	thought	thought
leave	left	left	throw	threw	thrown
let	let	let	understand	understood	understood
lose	lost	lost	write	wrote	written

Phrasal Verbs (Separable) and Their Meanings

*Don't forget to **turn off** the oven before you leave the house.*
*Don't forget to **turn** the oven **off** before you leave the house.*

Phrasal Verb	Meaning	Example Sentence
blow up	cause something to explode	*The workers **blew** the bridge **up**.*
bring back	return	*She **brought** the shirt **back** to the store.*
bring up	1. raise from childhood 2. introduce a topic to discuss	*1. My grandmother **brought** me **up**.* *2. Don't **bring up** that subject.*
call back	return a telephone call	*I **called** Rajil **back** but there was no answer.*
call off	cancel	*They **called** the wedding **off** after their fight.*
cheer up	make someone feel happier	*Her visit to the hospital **cheered** the patients **up**.*
clear up	clarify, explain	*She **cleared** the problem **up**.*
do over	do again	*His teacher asked him to **do** the essay **over**.*
figure out	solve, understand	*The student **figured** the problem **out**.*
fill in	complete information	***Fill in** the answers on the test.*
fill out	complete an application or form	*I had to **fill** many forms **out** at the doctor's office.*
find out	learn, uncover	*Did you **find** anything **out** about the new plans?*
give away	offer something freely	*They are **giving** prizes **away** at the store.*
give back	return	*The boy **gave** the pen **back** to the teacher.*
give up	stop doing	*I **gave up** sugar last year. Will you **give** it **up**?*
help out	aid, support someone	*I often **help** my older neighbors **out**.*
lay off	dismiss workers from their jobs	*My company **laid** 200 workers **off** last year.*
leave on	allow a machine to continue working	*I **left** the lights **on** all night.*
let in	allow someone to enter	*She opened a window to **let** some fresh air **in**.*
look over	examine	*We **looked** the contract **over** before signing it.*
make up	say something untrue or fictional (a story, a lie)	*The child **made** the story **up**. It wasn't true at all.*
pay back	return money, repay a loan	*I **paid** my friend **back**. I owed him $10.*
pick up	1. get someone or something 2. lift	*1. He **picked up** his date at her house.* *2. I **picked** the ball **up** and threw it.*
put off	delay, postpone	*Don't **put** your homework **off** until tomorrow.*
put out	1. take outside 2. extinguish	*1. He **put** the trash **out**.* *2. Firefighters **put out** the fire.*
set up	1. arrange 2. start something	*1. She **set** the tables **up** for the party.* *2. They **set up** the project.*
shut off	stop something from working	*Can you **shut** the water **off**?*
sort out	make sense of something	*We have to **sort** this problem **out**.*
straighten up	make neat and orderly	*I **straightened** the messy living room **up**.*
take back	own again	*He **took** the tools that he loaned me **back**.*
take off	remove	*She **took off** her hat and gloves.*
take out	remove	*I **take** the trash **out** on Mondays.*
talk over	discuss a topic until it is understood	*Let's **talk** this plan **over** before we do anything.*
think over	reflect, ponder	*She **thought** the job offer **over** carefully.*
throw away/ throw out	get rid of something, discard	*He **threw** the old newspapers **away**.* *I **threw out** the old milk in the fridge.*
try on	put on clothing to see if it fits	*He **tried** the shoes **on** but didn't buy them.*
turn down	refuse	*His manager **turned** his proposal **down**.*
turn off	stop something from working	*Can you **turn** the TV **off**, please?*
turn on	switch on, operate	*I **turned** the lights **on** in the dark room.*
turn up	increase the volume	***Turn** the radio **up** so we can hear the news.*
wake up	make someone stop sleeping	*The noise **woke** the baby **up**.*
write down	write on paper	*I **wrote** the information **down**.*

Credits

COVER

© Andrea Facco/Solent Media

ILLUSTRATION

© Cengage

iv (tl1) Look Foto/Aurora Photos; (tl2) © Graham McGeorge; (cl1) © Shawn Miller; (cl2) Xavier Zimbardo/Premium Archive/Getty Images; (bl1) Joel Sartore/Photo Ark/National Geographic Image Collection; (bl2) © Alexa Meade; vi (tl1) © John Matzick; (tl2) Hannibal Hanschke/Reuters; (cl1) Thomas Peschak/National Geographic Image Collection; (cl2) © Dylan Toh; (bl1) VCG/Getty Images; (bl2) Ciril Jazbec/National Geographic Image Collection; 2–3 (spread) Look Foto/Aurora Photos; 4 John Tlumacki/Boston Globe/Getty Images; 7 holgs/iStock Unreleased/Getty Images; 8 The Asahi Shimbun/Getty Images; 10–11 (spread) Alan Dawson/Alamy Stock Photo; 13 Krzysztof Dydynski/Lonely Planet Images/Getty Images; 14–15 (spread) Robin Hammond/National Geographic Image Collection; 16–17 (spread) © Graham McGeorge; 18 SVF2/Universal Images Group/Getty Images; 20 Worldwide Features/Barcroft Media/Getty Images; 22 © Ami Vitale; 24–25 (spread) Andrzej Wojcicki/Science Photo Library/Getty Images; 26 (t) (cl) Iurii Stepanov/Shutterstock.com; 28 © Dian Lofton/TED; 28–29 (spread) pixelfusion3d/E+/Getty Images; 30–31 (spread) © Shawn Miller; 32 shomos uddin/Moment/Getty Images; 34 (tl) Byba Sepit/DigitalVision/Getty Images; (tc1) Tom Brakefield/DigitalVision/Getty Images; (tc2) Douglas Sacha/Moment/Getty Images; (tr) Jessica Moore/Cultura/Getty Images; (bc) Scott Olson/Getty Images News/Getty Images; 36 Victor Tyakht/Alamy Stock Photo; 38–39 (spread) David Evans/National Geographic Image Collection; 41 VSanandhakrishna/iStock/Getty Images; 42 Steve Jurvetson; 42–43 (spread) Paul Nicklen/National Geographic Image Collection; 44–45 (spread) Xavier Zimbardo/Premium Archive/Getty Images; 48 Rica Santuyo/EyeEm/Getty Images; 50 Milosz Maslanka/Shutterstock.com; 52–53 (spread) Udo Geisler; 54 Annie Griffiths/National Geographic Image Collection; 56 © James Duncan Davidson/TED; 56–57 (spread) lisapresley/iStock/Getty Images; 58–59 (spread) Joel Sartore/Photo Ark/National Geographic Image Collection; 60 Stephen Wilkes/The Image Bank/Getty Images; 62 Volker Steger/Science Photo Library/Getty Images; 66–67 (spread) Lillian Suwanrumpha/AFP/Getty Images; 68 Mario Tama/Getty Images News/Getty Images; 70 AP Images/Steven Day; 70–71 (spread) © James Duncan Davidson/TED; 72–73 (spread) © Alexa Meade; 74 Harris Brisbane Dick Fund, 1948/The Metropolitan Museum of Art; 76 Tolga Akmen/Anadolu Agency/Getty Images; 80–81 (spread) Vincent van Gogh (Dutch, 1853-1890) Irises, 1889, Oil on canvas 74.3 × 94.3 cm (29 1/4 × 37 1/8 in.), 90.PA.20 The J. Paul Getty Museum, Los Angeles; 82 (cl) Historic Images/Alamy Stock Photo; (c) Album/Alamy Stock Photo; (bc) The Picture Art Collection/Alamy Stock Photo; 84–85 (spread) Michael Bradley/Getty Images News/Getty Images; 86–87 (spread) © John Matzick; 90 RioPatuca/Alamy Stock Photo; 93 Alfribeiro/iStock Editorial/Getty Images; 94–95 (spread) stockstudioX/E+/Getty Images; 96 Balate Dorin/Shutterstock.com; 98 © Bret Hartman/TED; 98–99 (spread) mdesigner125/iStock Editorial/Getty Images; 100–101 (spread) Hannibal Hanschke/Reuters; 102 Anthony Wallace/AFP/Getty Images; 104 Guven Yilmaz/Anadolu Agency/Getty Images; 107 Drazen/E+/Getty Images; 108–109 (spread) Betsie Van der Meer/Stone/Getty Images; 110 AdShooter/E+/Getty Images; 112–113 (spread) © Stacie McChesney/TED; 114–115 (spread) Thomas Peschak/National Geographic Image Collection; 116 golero/E+/Getty Images; 119 Digital Vision/Getty Images; 120 mansong suttakarn/Shutterstock.com; 122–123 (spread) Magdalena Adamczak/National Geographic Your Shot; 124 KatarzynaBialasiewicz/iStock/Getty Images; 126–127 (spread) Oto Chu Bordeaux/Bsip/Alamy Stock Photo; 128–129 (spread) © Dylan Toh; 130 Mark Thiessen/National Geographic Image Collection; 132 MyLoupe/Universal Images Group/Getty Images; 134 Bernardo Ponte/YourShot; 136–137 (spread) Funfunphoto/Moment/Getty Images; 138 (bl) Paul Fleet/Alamy Stock Photo; (bc) Georg.S.V/Shutterstock.com; 140–141 (spread) pictureproject/Alamy Stock Photo; 142–143 (spread) VCG/Getty Images; 145 Oleksandr Rupeta/NurPhoto/Getty Images; 146 Jianan Yu/Reuters; 148 Tom Stoddart Archive/Hulton Archive/Getty Images; 150–151 (spread) VCG/Getty Images; 152 Doublespace/View Pictures/Universal Images Group/Getty Images; 154–155 (spread) Joal van Houdt/National Geographic Image Collection; 156–157 (spread) Ciril Jazbec/National Geographic Image Collection; 158 Tim Jenner, 2009/Shutterstock.com; 159 John W Banagan/Photographer's Choice/Getty Images; 161 Robyn Beck/AFP/Getty Images; 162 Chris Hellier/Alamy Stock Photo; 164–165 (spread) loops7/E+/Getty Images; 166 Razvan Ciuca/Moment/Getty Images; 168–169 (spread) © Bret Hartman/TED.